DATE DUE

NEW BOOK TO BE
CIRCULATED BEGINNING

DEC 1 5 1977

Withdrawn

AP 1 9 '99

SEP 3 0 2004

10-11-07

SOVIET SPORTS EXERCISE PROGRAM

SOVIET SPORTS
EXERCISE PROGRAM

THE GOLD MEDAL GUIDE TO PHYSICAL FITNESS

NORMAN MACLEAN and BARRY WILNER
with DR. EARL HOERNER

DRAKE PUBLISHERS INC.
NEW YORK · LONDON

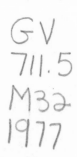

To Susie,

Who dreams of being another Olga Korbut.

Published in 1977 by
Drake Publishers, Inc.
801 Second Avenue
New York, N.Y. 10017

Library of Congress Cataloging in Publication Data
MacLean, Norman.
    Soviet sports exercise program.

    1. Physical education and training -- Russia
2. Exercise.   I. Title.
GV711.5.M32   796.4'0947   76-16367
ISBN: 0-8473-1309-3

Printed in the United States of America

AUTHORS' BIOGRAPHIES

EARL HOERNER

Earl F. Hoerner, M.D. is the chairman of the Amateur Hockey Association of the United States Safety and Protective Equipment Committee, as well as chairman of the American Society for Testing and Materials subcommittee F-8.15. He, along with Dr. Paul Vinger spearheaded the drive toward mandatory face masks in minor hockey and is presently hard at work setting up standards for the revolutionary facial protectors.

At one time, the main driving force in New Jersey amateur hockey, nicknamed "Mr. Hockey" in that State by many, Dr. Hoerner owned and ran the Essex Comets in the New York Metropolitan Junior Hockey Association. He is associated with both the New York Football Giants and the New York Rangers in an advisory capacity. An expert in both orthopedic surgery and physical conditioning Dr. Hoerner has established his own clinic in West Orange, N.J. where he puts to practical application the many aspects of physical conditioning he evolved from attendance at lend lease seminars in Sweden and Moscow.

Along with Montreal's Dr. Ed Enos, and Syracuse University's Mike Smith, Dr. Hoerner is part of the task force employed by Rangers general manager John Ferguson in attaining top flight physical and mental conditioning. Their revolutionary ideas, many of which are evolved from the Soviets, are now being adopted elsewhere in hockey and other professional sports in North America.

NORMAN MACLEAN

Norman MacLean conceived the idea of this book while covering the 1976 Winter Olympics at Innsbruck, Austria. The dedication, superior physical conditioning and scientific approach of the Russian athletes impressed MacLean, who had previously worshipped at the shrine of North American professional sports.

The writer of 23 previous books on baseball, football, hockey and basketball, MacLean formerly was the New York Rangers TV color analyst, and presently contributes to *The Sporting News, The Hockey News* and other national magazines. He covered the American League champion New York Yankees pennant drive, playoff and world series last year, sandwiching in coverage of hockey's Canada Cup, and then switching to the NFL, in assignments for the *Associated Press.*

MacLean, 45, is one of the founders of the New York Metropolitan Junior Hockey Association, and still serves as its Commissioner. He was associate public relations director and program editor of the Westchester Golf Classic for eight years.

Previous books published by Drake, by MacLean, include *Casey Stengel, The Hockey Quiz Book* and *The Basketball Quiz Book.*

BARRY WILNER

Barry Wilner is a member of the sports staff of the *Associated Press* in New York. As a freelance writer, Mr. Wilner has covered every major sport for a variety of sports publications. He has also collaborated on several sports books in recent years including the *Associated Press Sports Almanac,* for which he was associate editor.

CONTENTS

A Word about Measures

Russia uses the metric system rather than the prevailing one of feet and inches customarily used in the U.S. and Canada. Since some of the tables in this book are expressed in metric figures, the following conversions may be useful.

Metric Measure	American Equivalent
1 meter	39.37 inches
1 meter	3.28 feet
50 meters	164.0 feet
100 meters	328.0 feet
1 kilometer	3,280.8 feet
1 kilometer	0.62 miles
5 kilometers	3.1 miles
10 kilometers	6.2 miles

SOVIET SPORTS EXERCISE PROGRAM

CHAPTER ONE

Introduction: How the Soviets Became the Best

Since the close of World War II the Soviet Union has become the leading sports nation in the world. They have attained this lofty position in international sports because of their unique approaches to physical and mental conditioning, teamwork, and an unquestioning devotion to the Soviet way. This book examines the Russian systems of coaching, training, and participation and attempts to explain the key elements that make the Soviet methods superior to those used anywhere else in the world. And it looks at individual coaches and performers in the U.S.S.R., their philosophies and teaching methods, and how they contrast with North American systems.

The Russians didn't invent sports, although they might claim to have done so. But they have discovered methods that enable them to dominate international games. The Soviet Union practiced a policy of sports isolation for decades. Not until World War II did the U.S.S.R. join an international sports organization. They first entered the Olympics in 1952. But from the period beginning in 1949 and ending just prior to the Rome Olympics in 1960 the Russians made their presence fully felt in world athletics. A prime example of their success was described in the Soviet publication *Kommunist* and highlighted in Dr.Henry Morton's fine examination of the Soviet athletic system, *Soviet Sports:*

Soviet athletes in the past 10 years (1949-59) have set approximately 4,000 all-Union records, 700 of which were also world records. It is a curious fact that in 1948 Soviet athletes held only 18 world records and United States athletes held 56 in the listing for track-and-field events, cycling, shooting, swimming and weightlifting, while at present Russia holds 81 records and the United States only 52.

Soviet athletes have recently administered defeats to their chief rivals in athletics—the Americans—in track-and-field, wrestling, hockey, basketball, weightlifting, shooting, chess, skating, skiing and pentathlon....

Many of these claims are bogus, because Soviet teams met second-rate American squads. But in both Olympic and international sports the Russians are undeniably the best.

After World War II the Soviets did not plunge wholeheartedly into international sports competitions. In fact, Russian teams often were accused of ducking the tougher opposition due to their fear of failure and the resultant trauma that defeat would cause to the Soviet premise of superiority. Realizing the pointless nature of picking your opponents and avoiding the top competition, the Soviets began to come out of their sporting shell in the late 1940s. By 1951 they were prepared for Olympic competition and applied for entrance to the Olympic Games of 1952.

In 1948 the Central Committee of the Soviet Communist Party passed the following resolution, as outlined by Dr. Morton in his study of Russian athletics:

It is therefore proposed (by the various Soviet governing bodies):

To review the standards of rated athletes and masters of sports with a view to bringing them closer to Soviet and world records, and to work out standards for republic, territory, region records with a view to raising achievements to the level of Soviet records.

To publicize widely through the press, radio and movies all world records, as well as the best experiences of athletic training, to publish notebooks, handbooks, bulletins and yearbooks listing the best achievements in all sports in the Soviet Union and abroad.

To improve in conjunction with the ministries of education of the union republics the work of sports schools for youth.

To improve training methods; to provide greater incentives and

American Hockey Players, in Russia for Junior Tournament, look over Moscow skyline. The planned Soviet approach to sports conditioning far exceeds the last minute crisis approach of the Western World.

responsibilities to coaches; to assist them in coaching talented youths who show promise of breaking Soviet and world records; to take steps to train more coaches.

The final two resolutions are the most significant. Through a well-developed system of scouting and educating potential stars at young ages the Soviets have become a premier sporting nation. Their work in developing training techniques and in utilizing science and medicine to improve those techniques stems from the 1948 policy set forth by the Central Committee. The education of coaches until they are experts in their chosen professions also originated with the edicts of 1948. But winning is no longer the sole consideration in Soviet sports circles. The Russians are willing to absorb defeat in order to gain precious experience. They are never humiliated in defeat, and they come back the next time with added knowledge. It is a well-accepted axiom that you do not overwhelm the Russians more than once. Nor do you often beat them more than once.

After World War II the U.S.S.R. realized its goal of becoming a superpower. As the leader of the Communist world the Russians felt an obligation to excel in all areas: the military, the arts, science, and sports. It is a measure of the success of the Soviet programs that the rest of the world envies the Russian development. The Soviets are so far ahead of their competitors in training and teaching techniques that it will take years for them to catch up.

Throughout the 1950s the Russians concentrated on competition and on developing domestic programs. The accent shifted somewhat in the 1960s when Soviet supremacy in international competition became apparent. While the Russian sporting hierarchy did not deemphasize athletics on the international level, it did reemphasize the overall physical health of the general populace. In the 1970s both objectives have been reached—a healthy and progressive sporting population and continued success in the Olympics and other international events.

The Russian sporting background is not rich in 20th-century stars and folklore. Part of the reason for the intense concentration on sports today may be a desire to erase past mediocrity from memory. There is nothing better than a current hero to make people forget old heroes—or the lack of them.

During the Stalin years Russia existed in isolation. No one outside the country was aware that sports were being developed under a very careful system of recruitment and training. When the Soviet Union suddenly became a major contender in a variety of sports, the outside world was taken by surprise. Training for the Olympics began in 1935. For the first time athletics, including gymnastics, football, and boxing, were regarded as nationally important. After World War II the Soviet Union became a member of the National Sports Federation and the International Olympics Committee. In 1948 there were three million sportsmen; ten years later the number doubled. Since the 1952 Olympics at Helsinki Russian sports have gained tremendous momentum. After losing to the United States in track-and-field their desire to achieve international recognition became strong than ever. The Russians were trophy-hungry that year—they were climbing for the top, they wanted to be the champions of sport. Not only the quantity but also the quality of physical education for all Russians began to be stress-ed.

Since Russia is a Communist country, the government controls all aspects of the citizens' lives, including sports, in which organized participation is total. The government controls athletic training, the building of new clubs, medical assistance, mass-participation activities, and even publicity. Athletes are trained and looked after by the state from childhood throughout their lives, an unfamiliar procedure to other countries where participation in sports is a personal choice.

At one time Soviet sports successes surprised many people, but no more. Instead of downgrading the Russian system Americans should learn from their achievements. The American sports heritage is a rich and proud one, but this country would do well to take a lesson from the Soviet Union and develop a physically fit populace. There is no need to forget the past but no advantage in harping on it.

CHAPTER TWO

The Grass Roots: How and Why Russian Young People Become Sports Stars

While it is not true that Russian children are taught to run, jump, skate, shoot, ski, and swim before they can talk, such exaggerations are not that far out of line. In the Soviet sports system no one is too young to begin training for an athletic career. Just like the Wonder Bread commercials used to say, a youngster's formative years are of utmost importance. In the United States athletic training starts to lag behind when children are just graduating from building blocks or dolls to electric trains and more sophisticated games. Soviet coaches and talent scouts have already begun to select promising youngsters of the same age for their programs. Admittedly, nine-year-old children (the age limit set by the Committee for Physical Culture and Sports of the U.S.S.R.) rarely show the potential that would mark them as budding stars. But the Russian belief that a world-class athlete can be molded and created by beginning the correct learning processes at an early age seems to be working, at least for the Soviet Union.

Once again, it must be remembered that Russian children have little to distract them from becoming athletes-in-training. Luxuries such as toys and dolls, which seem to be necessities in capitalist societies, are not popular in a

Communist nation. The socialist environment encourages a youngster to look in other directions, especially in view of the scarcity of choices available to him. Many great honors are attainable in the Soviet system, none of which includes personal glory and fame for oneself alone. To represent the U.S.S.R., whether as an ambassador or an athlete, a scientist or a dancer, is the first priority taught to Russian children.

On national holidays athletes parade through Moscow's Red Square in as impressive a display as any seen during New Orleans' Mardi Gras or on Chinese New Year. To young, still impressionable children marching in such a parade seems like an impossible dream. When they are told that the dream can become true, that they can easily become a part of such spectacles, most youngsters readily accept the invitation. The learning process has begun.

If a child shows talent in a sport, it will not go unnoticed. Extensive scouting systems have been set up by the Russian sport schools. A representative of these specialized athletic schools will be alerted to the promising youngster, and an invitation to attend the school will be tendered. He will attend the school in addition to his regular classroom studies.

There are over 4,000 sports schools for children in the Soviet Union. Boys and girls between the ages of 9 and 18—limits set by the national sports committee but stretched so that even younger prospects may be admitted—are taught by expert coaches in any one of 33 sports. Many of the schools are restricted to one sport. Estimates that between 1 and 2 million youngsters attend these schools show their importance in the Soviet athletic system.

At the high-school level physical education is compulsory during the first two years and optional for seniors. By this time, however, non-athletes, youngsters who show little promise in sporting activities, have already been weeded out. Only the premier athletes remain to enter the sports institutes.

It would seem that the primary function of the Soviet sports-education process is to find the true potential for athletic stardom in each youngster and to train him in that specialty. Not so, according to the Soviets. Vladimir Brezhnev, head of the Central Army's hockey school, offers this analysis:

> We are interested in grooming replacements for our regulars. Most of our stars today began in our school, and we want to find more of them, keep the supply constant.
>
> But we are absolutely against youngsters sacrificing everything for

Olga Korbut, champion Russian Gymnast on the beam. The star of the 1972 Olympics, Olga has married and retired - but it was her pixie popularity and tremendous ability which "made" Gymnastics world wide. [Photo: Madison Square Garden Publicity]

sports. Sports are not professions in Russia. Sports should help children in school and life in general. They should steel them physically and teach them not to be afraid of anything.

If sports begin to interfere with a boy's studies, he is encouraged to give up hockey or track or basketball, to pursue his profession. But most of our boys easily combine studies and sports.

Imagine a fraternal organization in America—say, the Knights of Columbus or the Elks—establishing a sports school for youngsters in order to enhance their development and learning as athletes. Or a union, such as the Teamsters or the United Auto Workers, doing the same thing. Or one of the armed forces. And all to advance American sport in international competition under the guise of fully integrating education and sport. This is precisely what is done in Russia, although the Soviets have done a fine job in combining the learning process with athletic development and achievement.

Youngsters who are accepted by the sports schools have already shown excellent promise on the athletic field, even at the tender age of 9 or 10. They are the outstanding athletes, the ones who dominate their peers. They are rewarded for their physical prowess by an invitation to join the sports-school program. Few turn down such an honor. It may seem self-defeating to scout nine-year-olds. Many of them never advance beyond the norm despite early signs of potential. In fact, studies in the United States and Great Britain argue that a great majority of children do not reach athletic maturity before the age of 12 and may not be ready for full-scale competition before their mid-teens.

The Soviets believe otherwise. The coaches at the youth sports schools allegedly stress satisfactory grades in academic classes as a prerequisite for specialized athletic programs. But would they willingly pass up an obviously superior athlete whose grades were less than satisfactory? In the answer to that question lies the crux of the problem associated with the grass-roots movement in Russian sport. Despite the arguments to the contrary by Vladimir Brezhnev of the Central Army hockey school, many youthful Russians cannot handle the added weight of the sports school. And, in the case of the highly gifted athlete, special arrangements are made. Tutoring, a less rigorous educational program in the regular school, or a toned-down extracurricular schedule (in everything but sports, that is) prevent a promising athlete from slipping out of the coaches' grasp.

In many respects the system is already unfair. It excludes the late-developing performer (12 or 13 years old); it often places physical attributes and education ahead of the nonsports learning process; it endangers a youngster's interest in sports by stressing athletic activities at such an early age; and it stymies individual growth at a tender stage by grouping the superior athlete with other promising sportsmen, thus limiting his horizons and experiences to the sports world.

The not-so-superior athletes are also afforded a chance to learn and develop. The Pioneer Camps, usually run by trade unions, are set up for this specific purpose. They are the equivalent of American summer camps and essentially offer the same experiences to the youngster. The Pioneer Camps do not develop superior athletes simply because children who show extreme ability in sports are enrolled in the sports schools. The camps are really nothing more than vacation spots for city children, just as in the United States.

Parents of youngsters chosen for the sports schools are immediately rewarded. The family receives 60 rubles per month while their child is in training. The monetary windfall continues as the athlete progresses: 200 rubles for a junior national championship; 500, for a senior title; 1,000 rubles—1,000 American dollars—for an Olympic champion. Capitalism in action!

There are added incentives as well. If a youngster has adapted to his training and learned enough to become a world-class athlete, his rewards will continue to grow. A car is often provided, as well as what would pass for upper-class living accommodations in the Soviet Union. Global travel is allowed. A top-level sportsman in the U.S.S.R. is afforded all the luxuries earned by his counterparts in the free world. Since athletes comprise less than one percent of the Russian population, it is easy to see that the Soviet sports system is as capitalistic as any. Yet it works—very well, in fact. why?

The Soviet system is successful primarily because of the way that sports are taught to the young. The Russian sports schools are so thorough in preparing the students for athletic endeavors that their graduates, at age 18 or so, are experts in their chosen field. Perhaps these graduates are not the well-rounded people the Soviets would have one believe, but they are very sufficiently prepared to cope with their own worlds—hockey, soccer, basketball, or whatever.

What goes on in these sports schools? What is the teaching system? According to the Can-Am Hockey Group's study, it is as follows:

In practical terms, the sport schools try to teach children in groups of no more than 20. As children become more advanced in their chosen sport, they spend proportionately more time with coaches in groups of five. Classes are provided on a year-round basis with a preparatory period beginning in the fall and lasting several months, a more intensive, instructional period, and a one-month summer period designated to "get athletes up" for the fall classes. Athletes at the sport schools are supplied with equipment at no cost, nor are there costs involved with any of the major aspects of the schools activities.

Since the schools are run by trade unions or by army organizations, monetary problems are taken care of. And the government, which has a vested interest in these schools, is usually more than willing to help out if necessary.

Teaching in groups would appear to be self-defeating because the goal of these programs is to extract every bit of athletic ability from each individual. Each youngster would seem to need personal training programs and coaching. Even in a group of five the personal touch is minimal. Some Soviet psychologists and physiologists argue that early specialization in one activity—the sport in which the youngster excels—leads to one-sided physical development in the long run, a lackadaisical attitude toward actual game performance, and a superficial feeling that one has mastered the skills required of a particular sport. Yet, despite these negative factors the system works. Not perfectly, not without failures and dropouts, but with such a phenomenal success record that no other system in the world can rival it.

The main reason for its success is simple: motivation. The glory of representing one's country in international competition, the chance to affirm the Soviet system, and, although most if not all Soviet athletes would deny it, the opportunity to live a comfortable life in the U.S.S.R. Why shouldn't a child be pushed toward such goals? There are few others within reach in the Soviet Union. The life of a factory worker or farmer, compared to the glamour of athletic stardom, is enough of a contrast. But the Russian child-athlete is offered so much more in comparison to his less talented peers, who face a dreary future existence. If one follows the careers of two 10-year-old children, one a superior athlete and the other a mediocre one, the ensuing contrasts clearly illustrate the exalted platform, the pedestal on which a Russian athlete is placed. The situation is not noticeably different from that in North America.

The first youngster shows great promise in various sports and is placed in a sports school. He goes through the complex and rigidly structured learning

Ludmilla Turischeva, winner of the Gold Medal for all-around Gymnast in 1972 Olympics.

process and is expected to choose a specialization—say, track-and-field because he has excellent speed. For the rest of his life he will be a trackman. His entire life, at least until his career as a top-flight competitor is finished, will be devoted to learning and mastering the various skills of the sport. He will live a very closed existence, for few of the world-class athletes produced by the Soviet system are the well-rounded individuals that the Russians say they are. If he is successful, he will become a track coach or training instructor after he retires. The athlete who devotes his entire life to one activity in order to become a champion will most probably die the way he began as a 10-year-old—a trackman. His peer, a mediocre athlete as a youngster, will remain within the conventional Soviet education system. He will find his own niche outside of the sports world, perhaps in law, medicine, or science, perhaps in a factory.

The majority of the Soviet people resemble the latter example. Just as in any nation, the populace is not excessively talented, not world-famous, probably not even successful. Because one 10-year-old boy shows little physical prowess or potential while another exhibits tremendous promise, different ways of life are forced upon them. One will devote his entire life to sports, perhaps attaining a measure of glory, however temporary. The other, who at 20 or 25 might become a better athlete, will already have been eliminated from athletics because of his slow development.

Who is the real loser in such a situation? The Soviet Union would appear to be. The Russian ideal of a perfect blend of physical and mental capacities is far from a reality. They start children younger, but is that the best way? Are the Soviets getting the full potential from the vast resources that it is blessed with? The Russians do have more than their share of world champions, so one might say that they are the leading sports nation in the world and that they are doing things correctly. But is this the only way to measure the success of the Russian sports programs? Which is more important, the number of world champions that it produces or the total fitness of the entire populace?

It would seem that the Soviet system is faced with a paradox: on the one hand, develop the superior athlete to his fullest potential, afford the general public ample opportunity to stay fit, research the physical sciences for the ideal system pf physical development; on the other hand,exclude the late bloomer from the sports schools, limit his opportunities to exhibit superior talents at a more advanced age, forget about him. If he didn't have it at 10, he won't ever have it. This preposterous situation has become accepted in the

U.S.S.R. The world-caliber athletes produced in Russia are for the most part products of a superior system. The learning techniques, the application of science to sports, are vitally necessary to the physical development of the athlete. But so is the opportunity to prove oneself even if one is turned down for the specialized sports programs as a youngster. Once this is realized, the U.S.S.R.'s dominance of the fun-and-games world will increase.

Jack Ludwig, in his book *The Great Hockey Thaw*, written during the famous Soviet-Team Canada hockey series of 1972, takes an incisive look at the Russian sports system. His penetrating analysis expertly describes exactly what has been accomplished in the U.S.S.R.:

> I wondered, as I watched these children, whether our civilization had the intelligence and the freedom from self-blinding to look at what was being done in this place at this time...I wondered, as I looked at these children, whether some brilliant systems analyst might not have taken the techniques used in translating human motions into the machine motions of automation, and simply refined them, so that the human motions can be broken down into their constituent parts, and made into models for teaching. A humanistic, humane analyst might watch Jack Nicklaus, say, and combine his driving technique with the short-iron work of a Lee Trevino and the putting of a Gary Player, and so program a training regime for anyone who wanted to play golf well and gracefully. The same might be done in tennis—in any sport—not to produce world champions so much as to raise the level of everybody's performance.

This is precisely what seems to be happening in the Soviet Union. And it begins with the children, the athletes-in-training. The basic skills, considered dull and uninspiring by the western world, are taught to the youngsters. And retaught. And taught again until they are ingrained in one's performance.

At first the Soviet athletes seem to be an automated bunch, indistinguishable from one another in performance. But along comes a relative freewheeler—an Olga Korbut, for instance—and she captures the fancy of the sporting public. Yet for all of her remarkable, even revolutionary moves she is a champion because she is one of the automated Russian athletes. As a child she had to master the compulsory skills before attempting a backflip off the parallel bars. Her complete command of these primary skills, her ability to make them automatic in her performance, is the basis of the almost phenomenal acrobatics that she performs in competition.

This is a key concept that too few Americans accept. In this country it is considered important to break away from the crowd, to be distinguishable. In the U.S.S.R. individuality is tolerated only after an athlete has completely mastered the basics. The Soviet youngsters are better prepared to cope with changes in the norm. They always have the basics to rely on, whereas in most other societies children are taught to be original, sometimes at the expense of the fundamentals.

In his book Ludwig asks an important question, the answer to which he found to be elusive: "Is the point of the Soviet program the physical fitness of the Soviet youth or is it a recruitment operation to pick future international and Olympic stars?" While the latter is certainly a high priority for the Russian government, it does take pride in the physical well-being of its youth. Otherwise, why would it spend so much money, time, and effort to improve the physical prowess of its citizens? If Communism is inevitable, as the Russians have claimed for decades, then its people will develop physical fitness until they are the healthiest people in the world. And it all starts with the child.

The Soviet teachers realize the limitations of the body at such a young age. They stress only the exercises that the children are capable of doing. This viewpoint might be compared to that of the Little League: American baseball officials have suggested eliminating the curveball from the pitching repertoire because young, tender arms cannot handle the strain, but it has never materialized. Which makes more sense: allowing a young player to do as he likes throughout his formative years, with the possibility of permanent damage, or limiting him to activities that he is physically able to do without the threat of harm?

If a youngster takes up hockey, for instance, he is restricted from body contact for seven to eight years. The hockey program is geared instead to developing the muscles and the body to withstand the physical contact that will come later. Compare this to the North American boys' leagues, in which the skaters try to emulate their favorite N.H.L. or W.H.A. stars. If they see a particularly bruising, bloody game on television, the next day there they are, playing Dave Schultz or Bob Gassoff. The dangers in allowing such nonsense are obvious.

The same restrictions hold in other Soviet sports. Young gymnasts do not do backflips on the balance beam; water-polo players do not attempt over-

...nerican audiences were astounded by routine Russian gymnastic feats. Entire families ...ercise together on a regular basis. [Photo: Bob Glass]

the-head backhanders; and soccer players do not try midair slice kicks. Instead they learn gradually, working with the fundamentals until they are ready to take a shot at the more complicated maneuvers. In other words, no curves—just fastballs.

The grass-roots hockey movement in the Soviet Union is a source of great educational value. Any American team sport could be patterned along the same lines and would prosper. The young people are taught the basics before they are allowed to advance to overall skills such as playmaking, passing, shooting, or goaltending. And they are taught to promote the game of hockey, not themselves. Kharlamov, Tretiak, and Yakushev exhibit great personal ability, yet they think only of team and sport. And so do the kids.

When the youngsters work out at various clubs or organizations, they do not develop their own programs. One of the greatest misconceptions of the North American training approach is that an athlete in a team sport can prepare himself physically for competition. Anyone is mentally capable of psyching himself up in a proper manner, but, as the Russians have been telling the world, physical preparation is a group activity.

The youth of the Soviet Union learns this immediately. All practices are highly regimented: goaltenders do exercises designed for forwards and defensemen. The same applies to basketball: a center must learn ballhandling as if he were a guard. Everyone masters the training techniques, which are the same for all positions. The program involves a mass learning process of fundamental skills and preparatory exercises. And, compared to the alternatives in nonsports activities, it is fun.

It may be these alternatives that spur many of the youngsters. Involvement in sports is meaningful because an athlete's way of life is better, more prosperous. A hockey rink beats an assembly line in Canada or Kiev, in Manhattan or Moscow.

Initially there is little competition among the youngsters on one team. Each is concerned with achieving the prescribed goals set forth by the instructor: physical readiness, mental readiness, understanding of the fundamentals. As the athlete progresses, a sense of comparison emerges. This is natural in any society and in any activity. Before any bitterness can develop, however, the youngsters are taught the importance of the team. It is here that individuality dies, replaced by devotion to a common cause, loyalty to one's comrades, and obedience to one's superiors.

It is this subjugation of human emotions, this elimination of a reactionary outlet, that both advances and retards the Russian cause. Once a system has programmed a child, made his actions automatic—in essence, made him into a robot—his feel for a situation disappears. While he has a full command of the fundamentals to call on in a crisis, he does not have the emotional release to cope with this same crisis. The basics can take him very far, but, as international competitions have shown time and again, emotions can carry his opponent higher and further.

Of course, the team concept, the belief in working as a unit for a common cause, contributes much to the Soviets' success in sports. Rather than working alone or against a peer in order to outdo him, the Russian youngster helps his counterpart. Camaraderie takes the place of competitiveness: the only opponent is the high-jump bar or the balance beam. The kid standing next ot you is your partner. He may beat you in a race or jump higher than you, but he is a part of the team. If the team wins, nobody loses. The Russian youngsters understand this, or, rather, they are taught to understand it.

There are, naturally, some dissenting opinions on the Soviet athlete-producing system. Much of the criticism deals with the early age for starting training. Dr. Yuri Aivazian, head of the physical-education department at the United Nations International School and one of Russia's leading experts in gymnastics, has stated:

> Perhaps now we are starting the children too early. The girls sometimes start at 7 years of age and the boys at 8. I know that it takes until a boy is 18 before he can be a world-class gymnast. The girls are ready much earlier, which is why we can have an Olga Korbut or Romania can have a Nadia Comaneci, world stars at 14 or 15. But they may spend as many as 9 years before being able to compete internationally. Sometimes I think that is a long time to keep them interested.

Such may have been the case with Olga Korbut, the darling of the 1972 Summer Olympics in Munich. Her critical period occurred before the Olympics, so she was better able to adjust to gymnastics as her livelihood afterwards. "After she gave an exhibition at the world championships in 1970," reported *Soviet Life*, a popular English-language Soviet publication, "praise went to her head, she began to put on airs, ignored her teammates and trainers, and, in general, made herself objectionable."

A hiatus from gymnastics was needed to straighten Olga out. Unfortunately, much the same situation prevails with many young athletes in the U.S.S.R. and elsewhere. They are not properly equipped to handle instant fame and stardom. "In 1972, when illness and sickness prevented her from training," the *Soviet Life* article continues, "Olga began to understand the value of the support of teammates and coaches." She also realized that gymnastics was her life, the life that she had been trained for, the best thing that she could do, the best way that she could contribute to Russia.

Olga Korbut gives the impression that she has escaped the cold, automated stereotype of the Russian performer. She is a pixie, an entertainer, and the world loves her for it. But she is not really so different. Her performances are sporadically flamboyant, but it is her basic mastery of the sport that allows this freedom. To an American just learning to walk on a balance beam the backflip that Olga has perfected is a trick, something to impress one's peers. To Olga it is an exercise and a rather simple one at that. But it took five years of hard work at the fundamentals before she could include the backflip in her act.

This fact points up a very important difference between Soviet and American teaching methods. Many, perhaps the majority of, American coaches push their athletes too quickly in order to advance their own standing in the athletic community. If a coach's charge wins quickly, it enhances his reputation as a teacher and he gets more students. But rarely do these same coaches stress the fundamentals. They are looking for the shortest route to stardom for their athletes (and themselves). This is especially true in individual sports. Unless the athletes dedicate themselves to learning and mastering the basic skills, their chances of remaining at or near the top, especially in international competition, is slim.

In the Soviet Union, however, there are no shortcuts. As Dr. Aivazian states:

> The first thing we teach, in gymnastics or soccer or volleyball or anything else, is form. Good form and the basics of the sport. Of course, the coach has to know just what is basic and must be learned first. That is why they go through such a rigorous and lengthy educating system.
>
> In the United States, the gymnasts are taught tricks. Usually they are not ready for the movements they're trying and it hurts their whole performance and development.

They may not even have learned coordination and they still are allowed to do difficult things. This is wrong.

The whole process is a slow, cautious progression from the basics to the harder movements. This is necessary for the proper development of the athlete. One cannot be expected to score goals if he cannot skate. Or jump over bars if he hasn't learned the correct approach. It is the same for all sports.

Part of the problem in the western world is the motivation supplied to the youngsters. Says Dr. Aivazian:

Money should not be the reason we compete. In Russia, everyone participates for his physical well-being. The Soviet people want to be a healthy people. Sports are not a way to get rich in the Soviet Union.

If someone has ability, there is nothing to stop him from developing his skills. The government pays for the facilities, the equipment, the coaches, everything, in order to allow everyone to remain physically fit.

For a youngster to develop here (in the United States) is not so easy. He must have money for workouts and equipment and he must pay for teaching. That is taken care of in Russia.

CHAPTER THREE

Coaching

On a warm summer day in 1972 in Munich, West Germany, Valeriy Borzov proved that he was the fastest man on the face of the earth. As he crossed the finish line of the Olympic 100-meter dash, a slight smile crossed his lips. The Soviet coaches gathered on the sidelines frowned at such impetuosity.

Russian coaches, regardless of their sport, are an unusual lot. They are sculptors; they mold individuals with enormous raw talent into acknowledged superstars. But just as they scorn self-exaltation in their pupils, they refuse to share any of the glory. Still they are held in the utmost esteem by the athletes, their fellow coaches, and the rest of the sporting world. "Russian coaches are as highly respected as any people in the Soviet Union," says Fred Shero, one of North America's most acclaimed mentors. "To be a coach in Russia is a position of honor and they are treated royally."

For the most part the Soviet coaches prefer to remain a faceless breed. There are occasional rebels in the profession—people who are willing to give credit where it is due, which sometimes means to oneself. Anatoly Tarasov, perhaps the greatest Soviet sports coach, has written about his profession in a number of books. In explaining his coaching techniques Tarasov does not claim to have found the definitive way of preparing athletes for action. Instead he admits that, after careful study of hockey and other sports, the Soviets have developed their own system of training. "I have closely examined and analyzed North American, Swedish, Czechoslovakian, and Finnish hockey and have discovered many interesting factors which have then been utilized in our own national game," he writes in one of his published works, *Tarasov's Hockey Technique.*

Tarasov's approach to hockey is not unique in the Soviet Union. Practically every other team sport, from soccer to volleyball to basketball to water polo, is coached by men seeking new avenues to success. "We recognized almost immediately," Tarasov explains, "that our sports teams would be destined to remain a step or two behind their opponents if we simply copied existing procedures. So we have sought new ways.

"Now," he states with pride, "the situation has been reversed and other countries come to the Soviet Union to learn."

And not just in hockey, the number-one sport in Russia. Soviet methods in track-and-field, ice skating, gymnastics, soccer, and nearly every other sport that the Russians have mastered are being adopted worldwide.

Although the Communist system might seem to preclude the development of talent in individual-oriented sports such as track-and-field or weightlifting, the Soviets dominate these areas. The best weightlifters, gymnasts, and wrestlers in the world are unquestionably the Russians. Even a pastime as cerebral as chess is overwhelmingly dominated by the U.S.S.R.

Much of the reason for this supremacy lies in the teachers of such sports in the Soviet Union. While golf, tennis, and swimming, leisurely activities that glorify the individual more than most, (although Olga Morozova in tennis and the Women's 1976 swimming team are disproving this contention), may never prosper in the U.S.S.R. other nonteam sports do. The Russians demonstrate little interest in golf and tennis, rich men's games. Being landlocked and in a frigid climatic zone, swimming on a large scale is ruled out. So the Soviets have turned to the gymnasium.

"There is very little leisure life in the U.S.S.R.," says veteran sportswriter Will Grimsley, who has been to Russia four times and knows the intricacies of the Soviet sports system as well as any journalist. "At night, the family, instead of having a movie or show to go to, heads to the gym. Once there, they get into various activities. The father may wrestle, the mother will play handball or volleyball, and the children, who have already gotten a healthy amount of coaching in school, will be involved in any of a number of sports."

The youngsters, the source of future talent, are inspired by their parents. In the United States a father may watch his child play Little League once a week. In the U.S.S.R., however, the adults take part with their children. If a child asks his parent for advice in a particular sport, his father or mother can usually explain an exercise or a particular maneuver. There is thus a dual learning process in the Soviet Union: in the schools, where physical fitness is

iet coaches are required to continue their education with compulsory attendance at nics and Seminars.

stressed as much as the sciences and the arts; and at home, where the parent is often as knowledgeable as a coach.

It must be admitted that in the United States a parent who offers help to a child who is trying to master a particular activity, especially a sport, is considered to be interfering. Few American coaches like to see outsiders offer hints to their charges, and to the coach an outsider is anyone but himself. The Russians have no such self-defeating antagonism. Family participation is encouraged on every level.

Sports such as weightlifting, wrestling, and gymnastics are extremely popular because equipment is readily available and there is an abundant supply of qualified coaches. Weightlifting is a rather easy sport to teach. The maneuvers are very basic and do not change as the weight of the bar increases. Once a coach teaches his pupil the proper procedures, his work would seem to be at an end.

Although world-champion heavyweight weightlifter Vasilil Alexeyev, the World's Strongest Man, is now his own coach, he still thinks that proper coaching in his sport is a necessity:

> I could not coach because my own techniques would not work for others. In weightlifting, however, the athlete needs someone to boost his confidence and his knowledge.
>
> It is a very mental sport as well as a physical one. A coach is there to relieve much of the strain and to straighten out your problems.

Of course, Alexeyev is beyond that. He is the best—and he knows it:

> I try to give my opponents a shock, fool around and needle them. They're anxious and restless while I am relaxed.
>
> When I am ready, physically and mentally prepared, for some reason my feet turn cold. During the Munich Olympics, we performed in September in warm weather. But my feet were cold, which meant everything was all right. And I won.

Let's see a coach explain that!

Of course, a coach does more than explain and criticize the performance of his students. In the Soviet Union as in the United States, as Alexeyev reasons, he must lend moral support to his troopers. This is why Olympic all-around

With the Soviet, there is always someone in the wings. Olga Korbut was front and center, but Nelly Kim is top notch, too. [Photo: Bob Glass]

gymnast Ludmila Turischeva looks to her coach after each performance, as does Tatiana Averina, the Olympic gold-medal winner in speed skating, and even Nikolai Avilov, the 1972 Olympic decathlon champion.

A Russian coach is often harsh on his charges, scolding, warning, or even suspending a malingerer or complainer. But the student listens, whether he is an eight-year-old novice or a world champion. The coach's word is final. Either an athlete accepts this or he finds another coach. In the United States athletes often revolt if they feel that they have been subjected to excessive condemnation. In Russia they try even harder to overcome the deficiency. Perhaps it is this attitude more than anything else that has vaulted the Soviet Union to the top of the heap in international competition.

In other countries coaches are replaced or fired if they cannot keep up with the competition. American college and professional coaches are the best example of this win-the-title-or-else syndrome. In the U.S.S.R. coaches are rarely blamed for the failures of their athletes. Instead of firing the coach if a team fails, the players are replaced.

"Many of our players are very young," admits Boris Kulagin, coach of the Soviet national hockey team. "They are very difficult to reach." Kulagin may sound like your average, give-me-the-good-old-days Woody Hayes, but his complaint is just so much hot air, a product that sports coaches around the globe seem to monopolize. If a young player refuses to listen to his mentor, he is dumped from the squad. It is an honor in Russia to compete in sports on a highly organized level. Playing for a club team, representing your fellow workers or your neighbors or even your country, is a position to be envied. Few young Russians are foolhardy enough to challenge the establishment. Even fewer get away with it.

Yet Kulagin moans: "I have stomach troubles, and so would you if you had my troubles," he told *Sports Illustrated*. Kulagin coaches the Wings, another Soviet hockey team, as well as the national contingent. "The Wings are only in fourth place now and have shown a bad performance. I've got five newly marrieds on the team and they spend too much time with their wives and not enough with their hockey." Kulagin will not be fired if the Wings end up in fourth place this season—or every season, for that matter. His counterpart with the Detroit Red Wings, for example, would be lucky to last a full season in the same situation. But Kulagin is safe. His players are not.

Sports Illustrated's Mark Mulvoy visited the Soviet hockey factories last year prior to the series between two Russian clubs (Central Red Army of Moscow and the Wings of the Soviet) and eight N.H.L. teams. His observations on the Soviet coaches are quite revealing, not only about hockey coaches but about their peers in other sports:

> On or off the ice, Soviet coaches, with the possible exception of Boris Kulagin, hardly think or act with independence. They have all been programmed by the hockey federation and operate their training schedules and game plans with strict attention to the official federation-approved guidelines .... the coach who does not follow the unit system ... may not be very long for coaching.

Here lies the answer to the perplexing appearance that each Soviet athlete, regardless of his sport, presents to the world. The athletes learn from the coaches, all of whom fit into a particular mold. This uniformity is passed on to the performers, who are discouraged from showing even the slightest trace of humanity. For the most part the Soviet athlete, like his coach, is no more than a robot. Which makes it all the more refreshing when an Olga Korbut, a Valeriy Borzov, or an Alex Metreveli, one of the few Soviet world-class tennis players, hits the scene. A tear from Olga, a smile from Borzov, or a muffled curse from Metreveli lets us know that, yes, these people have feelings too.

Soviet coaches go through a rigorous, highly structured training procedure before they are certified. Since so much of the responsibility for Soviet supremacy in sports is placed in their hands, it is essential that they be experts in their fields.

A prospective coach must pass an examination in his sport—as must an athlete who aspires to the top level—as well as tests in Russian culture, history, and language. He is also required to master physics and chemistry before he can be admitted to one of the seven sports institutes in the country. These institutes are specifically concerned with training coaches. A potential coach is schooled in three areas: sports medicine, the psychology of sport, and the public sciences.

It sounds like a complex procedure, which it is. The coach who graduates from the program is a well-rounded teacher and leader who is comfortable in more than one sport. He is a scientist who understands the workings of the human body and is able to innovate with much success. The training period lasts approximately four years. During this time the prospective coach works directly with athletes in secondary schools as an instructor, usually for four months; as an assistant coach in high-level sports competition; and in study. Since most of the coaches at the top of the Soviet sports ladder are outstanding graduates from the institutes, it is only reasonable that they impart their knowledge to their charges, along with their own views on the game, and that the system prospers.

It is at the lower levels of competition that the Russian and North American systems are very similar. Coaches in the U.S.S.R. at these levels are volunteers who have had very little formal training, and are coaching because they seem to like working with young boys.... It is of some interest that boys involved in recreational hockey in the U.S.S.R. are considered "hooligans" because they have not attained the status of "elite athlete or student of sport."

The actual training of volunteer coaches is somewhat vague in the U.S.S.R., as it is in North America. Clinics and seminars are sponsored by the specialized sports institutes but are generally poorly attended.

In summary, the training of North American Minor League coaches is similar to that of the Russian coaches at the recreational level—whatever training there is is unsystematic and very poorly organized and regulated. *(Can-Am Hockey Group study)*

An important part of the coach's job is to educate the athlete on two levels. He demonstrates the job to be done as a whole and in part, and the athlete is expected to do the same while the coach corrects flaws in his performance. Two examples, one complicated—pole vaulting—the other simple—long jump—demonstrate the similarities in the teaching methods utilized by the Soviet coaches.

The long jump is one of the least complex events in sports. The athlete gathers up tremendous speed in his approach to the jumping line and attains maximum height and distance by stretching out the jump. The basic elements that must be mastered are: where to begin the approach, how much speed is needed, the correct way to take off into the jump, and the correct way to land to obtain the maximum distance.

The Soviet coach trains his pupil to analyze each step according to his capabilities so that he knows precisely what goes into the jump and realizes at each step that he is doing it correctly. If he makes a poor jump, he can pinpoint his errors and correct them the next time.

It is also important in the Russian system that the performer understand the whole skill. If the athlete thinks about each step in a correct jump, his

Olga Korbut, the darling of crowds in arenas throughout the world, is retired. Now a married woman, her place in the gymnastic spotlight has been usurped by Romania's Nadia Comaneci whose country also employs the Soviet conditioning methods. [Photo: Bob Glass]

concentration on the total skill will be diminished. He will have too much to think about. The coach's most vital function is to teach each individual procedure through practice so that the jump is entirely automatic. Only then can the athlete see the activity as a whole. If he masters the technique to the point at which it becomes automatic, then he can concentrate on the skill as a whole.

The long jump, with its four elemental steps, is taught in the same way as pole vaulting, the epitome of a multidimensional sports activity. The following procedures must be mastered:

where to begin the approach,
the speed needed during the approach,
how to carry the pole during the approach,
where to keep the eyes throughout the approach,
when to begin planting the pole,
how to plant the pole,
where to plant the pole,
where to focus the eyes while planting the pole,
how to let the pole propel the body upwards,
the position of the body at takeoff,
the position of the hands at takeoff and in the air,
when to push off from the pole,
the position of the hands at push-off,
the position of the body at push-off,
where to focus the eyes at push-off,
how to keep the pole out of the way of the body after push-off,
how to clear the bar, and
how to land after the vault.

Despite the complexity of the pole vault, Soviet track-and-field coaches teach it in the same manner as the far simpler long jump. The athlete practices consciously to master the individual elements of the vault; he develops a total understanding of the mechanics, which become automatic; he can then approach the event as a whole.

Practice is not the key to the Russian system. Although repetition is encouraged through practice, the Russians believe that using one's skills in a game situation will alone mold an accomplished performer. Soviet coaches also rely heavily on statistics. Every athlete has a performance chart, and his coach is supposed to know exactly why his charge was at peak efficiency one day but performed poorly the next.

As the Russians have discovered, however, statistics can be misleading. Even Valeriy Borzov may feel at his peak physical condition during a meet and yet lag behind the other runners. His workouts, designed to get him in top shape for the meet, may make him look invincible, yet he may lose. Why? Perhaps he is overprepared; maybe his mental outlook is dull; or he may not be as fast as his opponnets. It is the job of the Soviet coach to discover the reason and to remedy it as best as he can.

Some athletes aren't coachable, even in Russia. They do not fit the mold; they cannot be programmed to follow a specific procedure. Although the Soviets take a dim view of such individualism, it happens, and Borzov is a fine example. Just as Julius Erving or O.J. Simpson cannot be harnessed, neither can some of the top Russian athletes. Borzov is usually left to prepare himself (while his personal coach, Valentin Petrovsky, offers encouragement). He, better than anyone, knows how to get ready. In the U.S.S.R. independence is the greatest luxury afforded to a world-class athlete. It is a form of freedom, yes, but it is tolerated simply because no coach can accomplish with Borzov what he can do on his own. The same is true of Alexeyev and of Valeri Brumel, the greatest of all high jumpers.

CHAPTER FOUR

Physical and Mental Training

The Russians have integrated science, medicine, and athletics into a system of physical fitness that is superior to any other in the world. Muscle development, coordination, endurance, flexibility, and nourishment are categories to which the application of physics, chemistry, biology, and medical know-how has enabled each individual to achieve his maximum performance. For every sport Russian coaches and teachers have developed a specific regimen. Many of the programs and exercises may seem to have little to do with the particular sport—but they have everything to do with the development of the athlete.

In hockey, for example, off-the-ice training is emphasized. North American coaches believe that a player can be whipped into shape through on-ice training alone: rarely do they even set up what is called dry-land programs, although they are the heart of the Russians' superior conditioning. Soviet players may not lace up their skates for weeks; North American hockey stars either skate their way into shape or get away with what they can. If a North American player is off his skates for weeks, that means he is on vacation. The Soviets are not afforded the luxury of training on the golf course or at the beach.

The same holds true of other sports. How many athletes other than gymnasts work out on a trampoline? Very few, except in the Soviet Union. The trampoline is a popular training tool for every sportsman, from the gymnast to the soccer player, the swimmer, and the basketball player. The Russians also rely on different systems of weight training for all sports, even those that appear to have little need for strength, such as volleyball.

Unorthodox? Perhaps, but when one considers that these exercises are one of the main reasons for Soviet dominance not only in athletics but in dance as well—ballet dancers rely on the same methods to develop body strength and coordination—it is a matter of simple observation to note how well the system works.

Dr. Ed Enos, the director of the Institute of Comparative Physical Education at Concordia University in Montreal, studied in the Soviet Union at the National Institute of Sport and Physical Education. He notes that "The most intriguing sport story and the lesson we can learn from the U.S.S.R. is based not on historical, socio-cultural philosophy or ideological considerations but on the ingenious way science is practically applied in the Soviet Union at all levels and to every sport." Dr. Enos found that the application of science to sports training begins on the lowest level, with the young child, and continues throughout the career of a top-flight athlete. Scientific data were also used to develop the popular physical-fitness programs. "In Soviet schools," asserts Dr. Enos, "language, mathematics and physical education replaced the North American educational theory of the three 'R's' of reading, 'riting and 'rithmetic." If a youngster shows enough athletic ability to be accepted to a sports school or institute, a direct scientific approach begins in earnest. "The immediate and practical applications of the latest scientific findings are part of the everyday learning process of all students in the institutes," adds Dr. Enos.

Dr. Enos spotlights the career of a top-flight athlete in an article published in *Swimming World* (November 1975). In the specialized sports-training institutes a youngster's "strengths and weaknesses will be analyzed scientifically. Subsequently, a 48-month program with short, intermediate and long-range performance goals will be established." Contrast this with the same four-year period in the life of a supremely talented collegiate athlete in the United States. If his sport is track or swimming, he is encouraged to work out all year, but no specfiic instructions or goals are offered. Only while he is in training for his particular competitive season does the swimmer or runner have the guidance of a coach or tutor. Many American coaches do take a full-time interest in their charges and devote much of their own time to enhancing their mastery of the sport. But this situation is prevalent only in individual-performance sports such as track or swimming. What about the team sports?

Superior college and even high-school athletes think about professional careers from the outset. They are expected to follow the coach's instructions

Olga Korbut

and training programs. The coach, in turn, has to worry about maintaining a flow of talented personnel to his school, so he is often out recruiting in the off-season. The basketball or football player is more or less on his own from the end of the college season until spring practice begins. He is expected to stay in shape his own way, which is not the spartan life imposed on him during the season. In the U.S.S.R. the athlete does not have his own way. He trains according to his teacher's instructions all of the time. The 48-month program is exactly that—a full 48-month training session.

Dr. Enos describes a hypothetical case in his article in *Swimming World*. He follows the life of a boy named Ivan from his selection by a special sports school to international competition:

> Ivan's daily training schedule as a 14-year-old boy could total five hours in duration: a two-hour morning workout prior to his academic classes for the day; . . . immediately after school another two-hour training session; and possibly a third supplementary period in the evening.
>
> As one observes the young Soviet athletes' training—the science of sport permeates every facet. As an illustration, if Ivan is a track-and-field athlete, as he moves on from national to international and Olympic competition his coach will have a urine sample, an EKG and other data collected every 48 hours to analyze his physical conditioning, progress and performance. Science will be applied in the field as well as in the laboratory.
>
> If, for example, Ivan is a middle-distance runner he will train with a miniature EKG instrument taped to his chest—indicating to him and to his coach exactly at what heart rate he is working—and what is the best rate for him from which to derive maximum benefits during aerobic and anaerobic (with and without oxygen) workouts.
>
> His performance will be filmed with high-speed cameras and studied on a regular basis. Subsequently, bio-mechanic and cinemagraphic analyses may be utilized to help correct any deficiencies he may have in his form.

How can a youngster's development not be helped by such procedures? He has a set program to follow, his progress is checked every other day, and the program is altered to suit his physical development, capabilities, and weaknesses. His heartbeat is continuously checked, and a perfect rate of performance in relation to his physical condition is established. He has the op-

Coach checks athlete's pulse. All aspects of training are carefully checked.

portunity to watch himself in training and competition on film, something reserved in the United States for professionals and affluent college players.

Weight training in the Soviet Union is so important to the development of the athlete that it is always applied on an individual level. In a class of a dozen 14-year-olds each youngster has his own set of instructions and exercises, geared to his physique and to his specialized sport. If his sport is wrestling, for example, he is assigned weight work to strengthen his legs, especially in the knee, thigh, and shoulder areas, which are the focal points in the sport. All wrestlers in the program are given exercises to build up the knees, thighs, and shoulders, but none of them has the same program: even two 5'10", 14-year-old wrestling trainees have different weight-training programs. Through constant scientific data gathering the coaches can determine the amount of work needed in certain areas by each athlete and design the proper individual program.

Training programs involve other sports as well, and not only related sports—trackmen playing soccer or swimmers playing water polo but totally diverse ones—soccer players doing gymnastics, volleyballers playing basketball, hockey players shot-putting, archers playing handball to strengthen their hands and wrists, or figure skaters playing soccer to improve leg movement and enhance coordination and timing.

The two most popular warmup methods involve running and the trampoline. Various exercises are favored, including jogging through obstacles, hopping alternately on each foot, running backwards (popular with American football and basketball players), bringing the knees high up to chest level or the heels to the back of the legs, and sideways sprinting, which enhances lateral movement, an important facet of every sport.

The trampoline work has been considered too dangerous in the United States for a long time (although it was popular during World War II), but it is a mainstay of Russian preparatory programs. East German divers began to use the trampoline in 1953 to improve their timing and their spring. It not only enhances spring, which is very important to athletes involved in jumping events, but also strengthens the legs, especially the feet and the knees, two prime areas for injuries, and improves endurance. Trampolining is a tiresome and often boring activity—if an athlete can spend long periods on the trampoline, he tends to maintain interest in any exercise. The immediate sensation of climbing onto a trampoline is fear. There is little feeling of control—it is as if the trampoline propels one into the air at its will. Soviet coaches start youngsters on it early to overcome their fear. They believe that any reluctance will disappear if the athlete participates in the given activity.

Which athletes benefit most from trampoline training? Gymnasts, because trampolining is a part of gymnastics; hockey players, especially goaltenders, who need to return to their feet quickly; soccer players, who use the trampoline to strengthen their feet and their leg coordination; divers, who can simulate their skills on the trampoline.

The Soviets have also developed unique mechanical tools as part of their scientific approach to sport. One of the latest devices used for athletic training is a machine called an external-muscle stimulator. During a 1976 trip to the Soviet Union *New York Times* sportswriter Robin Herman visited Dr. Yakov Kotz, chairman of the physiology department at the Central Institute of Physical Sport and Culture in Moscow. Dr. Kotz invented the muscle stimulator and plans to mass-produce it so that "there are enough machines for everybody to use." At the time of Ms. Herman's visit Dr. Kotz was working with Soviet tennis star Olga Morozova, who was preparing for the Wimbledon tournament. Ms. Herman describes the procedure:

> Dr. Kotz placed small conductor pads first on Miss Morozova's ankles and later on both thighs, her right forearm and finally on her back. The pads were wired to a compact blue control box adorned with dials and indicators that sat nearby on a wooden chair.
>
> ...the machine pulsated an electric charge onto Miss Morozova's muscles, forcing them involuntarily to contract for a period of 10 seconds, once each minute. The treatment of each muscle included 10 such cycles or 10 minutes of alternating stimulation and rest.
>
> Thus far there are three machines (at Dr. Kotz's disposal) which have been used primarily to help an injured muscle repair itself and to prevent further damage, but Dr. Kotz acknowledges the possibility of general strength training for entire squads of Soviet athletes as more machines become available.

While some discomfort is involved in the procedure, it is well worth undertaking if it improves performance and eliminates nagging injuries. Olga Morozova swears by the muscle stimulator, one of the first such machines that the Soviets have allowed westerners to see and study. She explained to the *Times*:

> The first time I used this machine was a few years ago before

Forest Hills. I twisted my ankle and it was so big I couldn't play.

After a few times (treatments with the machine) I was able to move well.

She also pointed out that many of her cohorts, including Billie Jean King, who has chronic knee problems, would be helped immeasurably by the muscle stimulator.

Perhaps the most conclusive indication of the machine's effectiveness is the fact that Dr. Kotz attended the world ice-hockey championships so that he could treat any injuries incurred by the Russian players immediately. An interesting medical concept is involved here. Dr. Kotz believes that muscles begin to atrophy immediately following an injury and that treatment should not be delayed. The Soviet sports hierarchy seems ready to accept the theory and to allow Dr. Kotz to put it into practice.

An injured Soviet athlete, if his disability involves a muscle (or many muscles), would not be immobilized but would undergo immediate stimulation from the machine. Whether it works will be proven in the near future. If it does, the amount of time saved would be tremendous. A Valeriy Borzov could pull a muscle in training and would be back in training the next day rather than on crutches. But is there any chance of a recurrence—or continued recurrences—of the injury? Many western physiologists feel that rest and rehabilitation cannot be dispensed with in the treatment of muscle injuries. It will take a great deal of convincing to sell the American doctors on the muscle stimulating method.

Dr. Kotz's technique might be more readily accepted as a treatment for muscle atrophy caused by long periods of inactivity or the aging process. Dr. Kotz claims to have successfully treated such cases with muscle stimulation as a part of the rest-and-rehabilitation process rather than a substitute for it. But Dr. Joseph Goodgold of New York University's Rusk Institute expressed doubts about the entire method to Ms. Herman:

Electro-stimulation as a method of exercise is not...as safe as carrying out exercise by limb movement under voluntary control.

The intensity of the electro-stimulation can be strong and, if the limb is in the wrong position, can rupture the muscle or tear it off its attachments.

Dr. Kotz' work seems to disprove this contention, but it is doubtful that

Not all Russians are as acrobatic as this, but Acrobatics is a major participant sport in Russia. [Photo: Madison Square Garden Publicity]

the Russians would admit to a mistake; instead, they offer perfection and expect it to be accepted as such.

Dr. Kotz explains that the muscle-stimulation method calls into play "100 percent of the muscle fibers." Voluntary exercise can involve at most 80 to 90 percent. The machine has more preventive that curative significance. The Soviet approach to medicine in athletics is to develop training methods and devices that prevent sports injuries. American research is more concerned with treatment after an injury. The Soviet philosophy seems to be far more useful. If they can develop machines to strengthen the body and to drastically reduce the chances of injury, they will continue to dominate world sports. And American teams such as the 1976 Olympic track team will continue to suffer from the loss of a Steve Williams or a Marty Liquori, who do not have available to them the advanced medical technology that Soviet athletes now take for granted.

The G.T.O. program, (which means "ready for labor and defense") is a mass physical-fitness system ostensibly designed to keep the populace prepared for war or work. It was begun in 1931 to test a person's abilities in all-around sports activities. There are three categories in the program, the first of which is for teenagers (generally 14 to 16). Dr. Henry Morton, in his book on Soviet sports, asserts that this category concentrates on "morning calisthenics, rope and pole climbing, 60-meter dash, high and broad jumps, 50-meter swim, skiing, grenade-throwing and hiking." The same set of activities is performed at the next level, which is for young men and women in their late teens, with the addition, according to Dr. Morton, that "young men must fulfill small-caliber rifle firing norms." The final level is for supremely talented athletes in their twenties. Mastery of a motor vehicle, mountain climbing, and/or parachuting is required.

Physical-education methods in the schools vary slightly from the G.T.O. program. "The program for the 4th grade," writes Dr. Morton, "calls for marching drills, rope climbing, broad and high jumping, throwing small balls using the 'behind-the-back and over-the-shoulder method for distance,' skiing, basketball and the knowledge of at least 15 active sports." At 14 years of age the school system adds obstacle courses, trapeze and other gymnastic maneuvers, track activities of varying lengths and minimum times, and many team games and sports.

The Soviet people are in training even for their own amusement. There is a television show in Moscow that involves school children and adults in

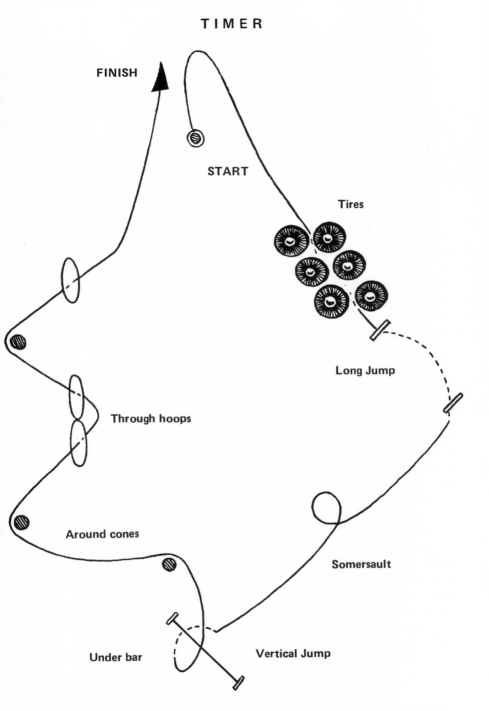

TIMER

FINISH

START

Tires

Long Jump

Through hoops

Around cones

Somersault

Under bar

Vertical Jump

Soviet Agility Run. This conditioning exercise is used on foot by Soccer teams and on ice by Hockey teams.

made-up games. The adults sponsor the games, providing whatever equipment is necessary—usually ropes, poles, stilts, and balls.

Since there are 210,000 sports clubs in Russia and over 50 million participants, formal programs are necessary to maintain the national health. Before an individual is assigned to a physical-fitness unit, he is given a full-scale medical checkup to determine his state of health. People are divided into groups according to their condition.

To make it even easier to participate in physical exercises, the Soviet government recently passed a ruling that all new housing must have sports facilities. What is included in these facilities depends on the size of the community: a skating rink, swimming pool, and gymnasium are common, but an extremely large housing complex often has soccer fields or even a stadium.

At work the emphasis on sports continues. Since many factories sponsor teams in the major Russian leagues, workers are strongly encouraged to become involved in athletics. A recent edition of *Soviet Life* explains the importance of sports programs in industry:

> Sports help on the job as well. Doctors and physiologists have begun to search for different occupational patterns of motion that will compensate for inactivity of one group of muscles. Statistics show that in factories where sports get big play, the incidence of ailments drops.

The Soviet Union is convinced that a sports-minded nation is a healthy nation, and they carry this philosophy much further than other countries: more people are involved in participant sports in Russia than anywhere else in the world.

The importance of mental training to the athletic program is not overlooked. The Russians stress a strong balance of physical prowess and mental capacity, reasoning that the mind is a powerful force that must be cultivated for proper conditioning. Dr. Ed Enos describes the mental-training program:

> The Soviet athlete can not call on any psyching procedures. Instead, the Russians work on demotoric procedures. By this, I mean the gathering of proper rest during a rest period.
>
> In North America, players rarely get the proper amount of rest

during times of inactivity. But the Soviet performer completely cuts off the outside. He ignores whatever competition is taking place and, instead, he concentrates on the fact that he is resting.

The Russian hockey player, for instance, will immerse himself in concentration on relaxing. Perhaps he'll take deep breaths. But, in between shifts, he thinks only of rest, no matter what happens on the ice.

Dr. Enos disputes the belief that Soviet athletes are passionless:

They can show plenty of emotion. Watch them during the Olympics, for instance, and you will see a number of displays of emotion, happiness or despair. They can be as excitable as any of our athletes, but they are culturally taught not to be demonstrative. That is why Olga Korbut went through a period of disfavor in the Soviet Union. She was too open for the Soviet coaches and sports regime.

There is no mental doubting of the procedures employed to train the Russian athlete by the athlete. They have to accept the methods. They do not question why a particular exercise is used.

Dr. Enos makes this assessment of the mental-training and data-gathering procedures employed by sports scientists:

The Russian athletes understand the importance of scientific data to their performances.

The Russians find psychological testing is a significant asset to placing a well-balanced team into competition. When they put eight rowers in a boat, they see who fits best together, who works best together.

For example, they do not want eight leaders in a lineup. They prefer to have some followers, so they will conduct a multitude of psychological tests to determine the mental makeup of the athletes.

It is good psychology to realize that the eight best physical specimens do not win the race. A proper mixture, which may even include some physiologically inferior performers, is required for a winning team.

CHAPTER FIVE

Soviet Physical-Fitness Tests

A new physical-fitness program, the P.W.D. (Prepared for Work and Defense) was instituted in 1972 to replace the original G.T.O. system. The stated aims of the P.W.D. are to assist the morale and spiritual development of the Soviet people, to encourage all-round harmony, to maintain good health and normal activity for many years, and to prepare people for productive labor and defense of the homeland. The overall purpose is to bring physical culture into the everyday life of people at all age levels in order to develop mass sport and find top athletes.

Physical culture is considered essential to the total education of Soviet youth, who are intellectually trained in Communist ideals and should be physically strong in order to work for and defend their country. Physical culture encourages moral, intellectual, and aesthetic development of the individual as well as his physical development.

The principle of *massovost* (mass participation) is absolutely essential for the development and existence of *masterstvo* (proficiency and achievement), for the more people who participate in sports programs at all levels, the easier it is to find future top athletes and the more athletes there will be in the top competitive levels.

The broad foundation of the *massovost* program is provided by the national-physical fitness and sports-awards systems, the physical-culture *kollektivs*, and the organized mass-participation events, such as exercise and sports demonstrations, excursions, marches, festivals, and competitions, all of which are held at regular intervals. Sports festivals, called *spartakiads*, are held at every level for school children, sport societies, and national summer and winter exhibitions. The most elaborate and massive are the all-union *spartakiads*, which are held every four years in the year preceding the Olympic Games. In the simpler stages the competitions are open to all, and the winners of the competitions may progress upward through the city, district, and republic levels to the finals at the national level. In 1967 80 million participated at the grass-roots level, and 16,138 in the finals.

HOCKEY GROUPINGS OF THE CENTRAL RED ARMY CLUB [1]

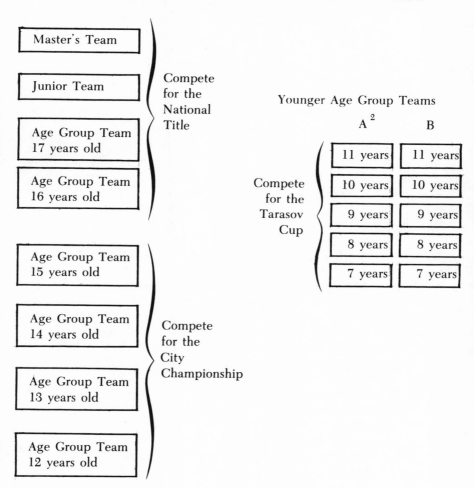

[1] Each team has 30 players with 5 units of 5, and 5 goalies. Special goaltending coaches are assigned to each team.

[2] A Teams are made up of players who have been at the specialized schools longer than the players on the B Teams.

GENERAL CHARACTERISTICS AND
DEVELOPMENTAL SKILL TEACHING

YEARS OF AGE

	7 - 11	12 - 14	15 +
GENERAL	- big muscles, gross - motor development - concrete thinking	strengthening of muscles and nervous connections, functional disharmony, skill not stable, ability to analyze, abstract thinking	critical analysis, physical training
PHYSICAL TRAINING	- all-around development, (games, relays, acrobatics, soccer etc) - flexibility and agility	all-around development, emphasis on strength and speed	special emphasis on strength and stamina
TECHNICAL	- test times on drills and skills, expose to various game situations - left and right drills	- all game situations - measuring drills and skills	-measure skills and drills at high speeds, accuracy, complex skills
TACTICAL	- development of attention - sight memory - orientation - individual tactics - learning simple combinations	- complex skills - group activities - mastering mechanical aspects of skills (not just doing but also knowing why) - complex individual activities such as fakes and dekes	-individual and group tactics -defensive positions specialized -options of defensive and offensive team play

First stage: boys and girls 10 to 11 and 12 to 13
P.W.D. (Prepared For Work and Defense)

Events	BOYS 10 to 11 Silver	BOYS 10 to 11 Gold	BOYS 12 to 13 Silver	BOYS 12 to 13 Gold	GIRLS 10 to 11 Silver	GIRLS 10 to 11 Gold	GIRLS 12 to 13 Silver	GIRLS 12 to 13 Gold
1. Running: 30m (seconds)	5.8	5.2	-	-	6.0	5.4	-	-
60m (seconds)	-	-	10.0	9.2	-	-	10.2	9.6
2. Long jump: cm	310	340	340	380	260	300	300	350
3. High jump: cm	95	105	105	115	85	95	100	110
4. Throwing (tennis ball): m	30	35	35	40	20	23	23	26
5. Swimming: (no time limit):m	25	-	50	-	25	-	50	-
.50m (minutes) and (seconds)	-	1.20	-	1.05	-	1.30	-	1.15
6. Skiing: 1km (minutes) and (seconds)	8.00	7.30	-	-	8.30	8.00	-	-
2km (minutes) and (seconds)	-	-	14.00	13.00	-	-	16.30	15.30
In snowless areas:								
Bicycling: 5km (minutes) or	16	15	15	14	19	18	18	17
Cross-country running: m	500	1000	1000	1500	300	500	500	1000
Chin-ups (full extension)	3	5	5	7	-	-	-	-
Rope climbing with feet: m	-	-	-	-	2.50	2.80	2.80	3.50

All seven silver standards must be passed to qualify for a silver pin; a minimum of five gold and two silver standards, for a gold pin.

Target: to be bold, daring and shrewd.
Aim:　　basic motor skills; discovery of main sports interests.

For the first stage there are two norms. A student may choose his preference for the gold pin only.

First stage: alternate norm

EVENTS	BOYS 10 to 11	BOYS 12 to 13	GIRLS 10 to 11	GIRLS 12 to 13
1. Run: 80m	4 obstacles	5 obstacles	3 obstacles	4 obstacles
2. Gymnastics	3 events	4 events	2 events	3 events
3. Hiking: km	5-6	specified course	5-6	specified course
4. Shooting	-	basic procedures	-	basic procedures
5. Skating:				
100m (seconds)	20	18	22	20
6. Participation				
in Sports Games	5	8	5	8

Second stage: boys and girls 14 to 15

Events	BOYS		GIRLS	
	Silver	Gold	Silver	Gold
Running: 60m (seconds)	9.2	8.4	10.0	9.4
Cross-country: 300m (minutes, seconds)	-	-	1.0	0.55
500m (minutes, seconds)	1.45	1.30	-	-
or				
Skating: 300m (minutes, seconds)	0.58	0.50	1.05	1.00
Long jump: cm or	390	450	310	360
High jump: cm	120	130	105	110
Tennis-ball throw: m	38	46	25	30
Skiing: 2km (minutes)	-	-	15	14
3km (minutes, seconds)	17.3	16.3	-	-
In snowless areas:				
Fast walk: 1km (minutes, seconds)	-	-	5.20	5.00
2km (minutes) or	10	9	-	-
Cycling: 5km (minutes)	-	-	15	14
10km (minutes)	28	26	-	-
Swimming: 50m (minutes, seconds)	1.00	0.50	1.10	1.00
Chin-ups (no time limit) or	6	8	-	-
Bar pull-over	2	3	-	-
Hiking: km	12	16	12	16
All-union classification	-	II-III	-	II-III

For the silver pin all standards are required; for the gold pin, at least six gold and the rest silver, including standard

Target: ready to replace their elders.
Aim: further development of physical fitness.

Third stage: boys and girls 16 to 18

Events	BOYS		GIRLS	
	Silver	Gold	Silver	Gold
1. Run: 100m (seconds)	14.2	13.5	16.2	15.4
2. Cross-country: 500m (minutes, seconds)	-	-	2.0	1.5
1000m (minutes, seconds) or	3.3	3.2	-	-
Skating: 500m (minutes, seconds)	1.25	1.15	1.3	1.2
3. Long jump: cm or	440	480	340	375
High jump: cm	125	135	105	115
4. Grenade throw: 500 g (m)	-	-	21	25
700 g (m) or	35	40	-	-
Shot put: 4kg, (m)	-	-	6.0	6.8
5 kg, (m)	8	10	-	-
5. Skiing: 3km (minutes)	-	-	20	18
5km (minutes)	27	25	-	-
10km (minutes)	57	52	-	-
In snowless areas:				
Fast walking: 3km (minutes)	-	-	20	18
6km (minutes) or	35	32	-	-
Cycling: 10km (minutes)	-	-	30	27
20km (minutes)	50	46	-	-
6. Swimming: 100m (minutes, seconds)	2.00	1.45	2.15	2.00
without time limit (m)	200	-	100	-
7. Chin-ups or	8	12	-	-
Pull-over	3	4	-	-
Bench push-ups	-	-	10	12
8. Shooting: 25m (out of 50) or	33	40	30	37
50m (out of 50)	30	37	27	34
9. Hiking	1 trip of 20km or 2 trips of 12km	1 trip of 25km or 2 trips of 12km	1 trip of 20km or 2 trips of 12km	1 trip of 25 km or 2 trips of 12km
10. Classification in any of the following: Car driving, motorcycle, parachuting, pentathlon, orienteering and	-	II	-	III
all-union classification	-	II	-	II

For the silver pin, all norms are required; for the gold pin, 7 gold and 2 silver, pl
norm 10.

Target: **strength and courage.**

Fourth stage: men 19 to 39 and women 19 to 34

Events	MEN Silver	Gold	Silver	Gold	WOMEN Silver	Gold	Silver	Gold
1. Run: 100m (seconds)	14.0	13.0	15.0	14.0	16.0	15.2	17.0	16.0
2. Cross-country:								
500m (minutes, seconds) or	-	-	-	-	2.0	1.45	2.1	2.0
1000m (minutes, seconds) or	3.2	3.1	3.45	3.3	4.3	4.1	5.0	4.3
3000m (minutes, seconds)	11.0	10.3	11.3	11.0	-	-	-	-
3. High jump: cm or	130	145	125	130	110	120	105	110
Long jump	460	500	400	460	350	380	320	350
4. Grenade throw: 500 g (m)	-	-	-	-	23	27	20	23
700 g (m) or	40	47	35	40	-	-	-	-
Shot put: 4kg (m)	-	-	-	-	6.5	7.5	6.2	6.5
7.257 kg (m)	7.5	9.0	6.5	7.5	-	-	-	-
5. Skiing: 3km (minutes) or	-	-	-	-	19	17	21	19
5 km (minutes) or	25	24	30	26	35	33	38	35
10 km (minutes)	54	50	-	-	-	-	-	-
In snowless areas:								
Fast walk: 3km (minutes)	-	-	-	-	19	17	21	19
6km (minutes) or	36	33	38	36	-	-	-	-
Cycling: 10km (minutes)	-	-	-	-	28	25	30·	27.
20km (minutes)	46	43	48	46	-	-	-	-
6. Swimming:								
100m (minutes, seconds) or	2.05	1.5	2.15	2.05	2.2	2.0	2.3	2.2
without time limit (m)	200	-	150	-	150	-	100	-
7. Chin-ups: weight up to 70kg	9	13	6	9	-	-	-	-
weight over 70 kg or	7	11	4	7	-	-	-	-
Military press to: of own								
weight: over 70	55%	75%	50%	55%	-	-	-	-
up to 70kg	65%	85%	60%	65%	-	-	-	-
Push-ups or	-	-	12	14	12	14	8	10
Sit-ups	-	-	-	-	40	50	30	40
8. Shooting: 25m (out of 50)	37	43	35	40	37	43	35	37
50m (out of 50) or	34	40	34	37	-	-	-	-
Small-caliber: 100m								
(out of 100)	70	75	60	65	-	-	-	-
9. Hiking	1	1	1	1				
	time	time	time	time				
	25km	30km	20km	25km				
	(same as for the men)							
	2	2	2	2				
	times	times	times	times				
	15km	20km	12km	15km				
10. All-union sport classification	-	II	-	-	-	II	-	

All norms are required for silver pin; 7 gold and 2 silver, for gold pin, plus norm 10.
Target: physical perfection (to be as fit as possible).

Fifth stage: men 40 to 60 and women 35 to 55

Events	MEN Gold	MEN Gold	WOMEN Gold	WOMEN Gold
1. Run: 60m (seconds)	12.0	-	12.8	-
Fast walk: 200m (minutes, seconds)	-	-	-	1.20
400m (minutes, seconds)	-	2.50	-	-
2. Cross-country: 300m (minutes, seconds)	-	-	1.25	-
800m (minutes, seconds) or	3.15	-	-	-
Jogging: (minutes)	20	15	110	8
3. Standing long jump: cm	190	170	150	130
4. Grenade throw: 500 g (m)	-	-	18	-
700 g (m) or	32	-	-	-
Shot put: 4kg (m)	-	-	5.50	-
7.257kg (m) or	6.20	-	-	-
Medicine-ball put: 2kg (m)	-	8	-	6
5. Skiing: 2km (minutes)	-	-	18	without time limit
5km (minutes)	35	without time limit	-	-
In snowless areas:				
Walking or running: 3km, (minutes)	-	-	25	without time limit
5km (minutes) or	40	without time limit	-	-
Cycling: 5km (minutes)	-	-	20	-
10km (minutes)	40	-	-	-
6. Swimming (without time limit)	100	50	100	50
7. Bench push-ups	10	8	6	4
8. Shooting (small-caliber) 25m (out of 50)	34	-	-	-
9. Hiking: km	20	10	20	10

All 9 norms are required for gold pin.

Target: to be cheerful, jolly, and healthy.
Aim: to maintain good health and physical fitness for a long time.

Stage 1: Brave and Agile (10 to 13 years)

Requirements
. Have an understanding of physical culture and sport in the U.S.S.R.
. Fulfil personal and community hygiene requirements.
. Know the fundamentals of civil defense and wear a gas mask for 30 minutes.
. Be able to explain and perform the morning exercises.

Exercises and Norms

Exercises	BOYS				GIRLS			
	10-11		12-13		10-11		12-13	
	Silver	Gold	Silver	Gold	Silver	Gold	Silver	Gold
. Run:								
30m (seconds)	5.8	5.2	-	-	6.0	5.4	-	-
60m (seconds)	-	-	10.0	9.2	-	-	10.2	9.6
2. Long jump: cm	310	340	340	380	260	300	300	350
3. High jump: cm	95	105	105	115	85	95	100	110
4. Tennis-ball throw: m	30	35	35	40	20	23	23	26
5. Swimming:								
m (time not calculated)	25	-	50	-	25	-	50	-
6. Swimming:								
50m (minutes, seconds)	-	1.20	-	1.05	-	1.30	-	1.15
7. Skiing: 1km (minutes, seconds)	8.00	7.30	-	-	8.30	8.00	-	-
2 km (minutes, seconds)	-	-	14.00	13.00	-	-	16.30	15.30
In snowless areas:								
Cycling: 5km (minutes) or	16	15	15	14	19	18	18	17
Cross-country: m (time not calculated)	500	1000	1000	1500	300	500	500	1000
8. Pull-ups (times) or	3	5	5	7	-	-	-	-
Rope climbing with aid of legs	-	-	-	-	2.50	2.80	2.80	3.50

For a gold award at least five gold norms and two silver norms are required, as well as the requirements from the choice-items section. (10 to 11 years, two chosen areas, 12 to 13 years three areas).

Choice Section

		BOYS				GIRLS		
1. Hurdles: 80m	-	4	-	5	-	3	-	4
2. Gymnastic apparatus (types)	-	3	-	4	-	2	-	3
3. Hiking: km	-	5-6	-	Young Tourist	-	5-6	-	Young Tourist
4. Shooting	-	-	-	Young Shooter	-	-	-	Young Shooter
5. Skating: 100m (seconds)	-	20	-	18	-	22	-	20
6. Participation in sports competition (games)	-	5	-	8	-	5	-	8

Stage II: The Rising Sports Generation (14 to 15 years)
Requirements: same as stage I.

Exercises and Norms

Exercises	BOYS		GIRLS	
	Silver	Gold	Silver	Gold
1. Run: 60m (seconds)	9.2	8.4	10.0	9.4
2. Cross-country: 300m (minutes, seconds)	-	-	1:00	0:5!
500m (minutes, seconds)	1:45	1:30	-	-
In snowy areas:				
Skating: 300m (minutes, seconds)	0:58	0:50	1:05	1:00
Long jump: cm or	390	450	310	360
High jump: cm	120	130	105	110
4. Tennis-ball throw: m	38	46	25	30
5. Skiing: 2km (minutes)	-	-	15	14
3km (minutes, seconds)	17:30	17:30	-	-
In snowless areas:				
Fast walk: 1km (minutes, seconds)	-	-	5.20	5.0(
2km (minutes, seconds) or	10	9	-	-
Cross-country cycling: 5km (minutes)	-	-	15	14
10km (minutes)	28	26	-	-
6. Swimming: 50m (minutes, seconds)	1:00	0:50	1:10	1:0(
7. Pull-ups (times) or	6	8	-	-
Pull-ups with weight or with turn	2	3	-	-
Pushups on gym bench in resting position (times)	-	-	8	10
8. Hiking: km	12	16	12	16(
9. Classification in desired sport	-	II-III youth	-	II-I] you'

In order to receive the gold award for this level, it is necessary to complete at leas
gold norms and two silver norms, not counting exercise.

Stage III: Strength and Courage (16 to 18 years)

quirements: same as Stage I except that the gas mask must be worn for 1 hour and
n must master one of the following—the elementary military-instruction program
cluding defense against mass-destruction weaponry), the Almavu specialized
paratory courses, or an applied-science specialty.

Exercises and Norms

	BOYS		GIRLS	
	Silver	**Gold**	**Silver**	**Gold**
Run: 100m (seconds)	14.2	13.5	16.2	15.4
Cross-country: 500m (minutes, seconds)	-	-	2:00	1:50
1000m (minutes, seconds)	3:30	3:20	-	-
In snowy regions:				
Skating: 500m (minutes, seconds)	1:25	1:15	1:30	1:20
Long jump: cm or	440	480	340	375
High jump: cm	125	135	105	115
Grenade throw 500g (m)	-	-	21	25
700g (m) or	35	40	-	-
Shot-put: 4kg (m)	-	-	6.00	6.80
5kg (m)	8	10	-	-
Skiing: 3km (minutes)	-	-	20.	18
5km (minutes) or	27	25	-	-
10km (minutes)	57	52	-	-
In snowless regions:				
Fast walk: 3km (minutes)	-	-	20	18
6km (minutes) or	35	32	-	-
Cross-country cycling: 10km (minutes)	-	-	30	27
20km (minutes)	50	46	-	-
Swimming: 100m (minutes, seconds)	2:00	1:45	2:15	2:00
Pull-ups (times) or	8	12	-	-
Pull-ups with weight or with turn	3	4	-	-
Push-ups on gym bench				
from resting position (times)	-	-	10	12
Pistol Shooting: 25m (hits) or	33	40	30	37
50m (hits) or	30	37	27	34
military training program	satis.	good	satis.	good
Hiking: 20km (times)	1	-	1	-
12km (times)	2	-	2	-
25km (times)	-	1	-	1
15km (times)	-	2	-	2
0. Sports classification:				
auto, motorboating, motorcycling, gliding, parachuting, helicopter, underwater, multiple-sea sports, biathlon, modern all-around shooting, radio, orienteering, wrestling (one area) boxing	-	III	-	III
any other chosen sport area	-	II	-	II

n order to receive a gold award in this level, at least seven gold norms and two silver
norms are required, not counting exercise 10. Girls may complete the preparations for
a sanitary squad to satisfy exercise 10.

Stage IV: Physical Perfection (men to 39 years, women 19 to 34 years)
Requirements: same as stage III.

Exercises and Norms

| | MEN | | | | WOMEN | | | |
| | 19-28 | | 29-39 | | 19-28 | | 29-39 | |
Exercises	Silver	Gold	Silver	Gold	Silver	Gold	Silver	G
1. Run: 100m (seconds)	14.0	13.0	15.0	14.0	16.0	15.2	17.0	16.
2. Cross-country:								
500m (minutes, seconds) or	-	-	-	-	2:00	1:45	2:10	2:0
1000m (minutes, seconds) or	3:20	3:10	3:45	3:30	4:30	4:10	5:00	4:3
3000m (minutes, seconds)	11:00	10:30	11:30	11:00	-	-	-	-
3. High jump: cm or	130	145	125	130	110	120	105	11
Long jump: cm	460	500	400	460	350	380	320	33
4. Grenade throw: 500g (m)	-	-	-	-	23	27	20	2
700g (m) or	40	47	35	40	-	-	-	-
Shot put: 4kg (m, cm)	-	-	-	-	6.50	7.50	6.20	6.5
7.257kg (m, cm)	7.50	9.00	6.50	7.50	-	-	-	-
5. Skiing: 3km (minutes) or	-	-	-	-	19	17	21	1
5km (minutes) or	25	24	30	26	35	33	38	3
10km (minutes)	54	50	-	-	-	-	-	-
In snowless regions:								
Fast walk: 3km (minutes)	-	-	-	-	19	17	21	1
6km (minutes) or	36	33	38	36	-	-	-	-
Cross-country cycling:								
10km (minutes)	-	-	-	-	28	25	30	2
20km (minutes)	46	43	48	46	-	-	-	-
6. Swimming:								
100m (minutes, seconds	2:05	1:50	2:15	2:05	2:20	2:00	2:30	2:2
7. Pull-ups (times)								
body weight to 70kg	9	13	6	9	-	-	-	-
body weight over 70kg or	7	11	4	7	-	-	-	-
Bar pushing from chest								
(% of body weight)								
Body weight to 70kg	55	75	50	55	-	-	-	-
Body weight over 70kg or	65	85	60	65	-	-	-	-
Push-ups on gym bench								
in resting position (times) or	-	-	12	14	12	14	8	1
Sit-ups with legs fixed and								
hands behind neck (times)	-	-	-	-	40	50	30	4
8. Pistol shooting: 25m (hits)	37	43	35	37	37	43	35	3
9. Hiking: 1 hike of	25km	30km	20km	25km	25km	30km	20km	2
or 2 hikes of	15km	20km	12km	15km	15km	20km	12km	1
10. Sports Classification								
in any sport	-	11	-	-	-	11	-	-

Stage V: Vigor and Health (men 40 to 60 years, women 35 to 55 years)
Requirements: Same as Stage I.

Exercises and Norms

Exercises	MEN		WOMEN	
	40-49	50-60	35-45	45-55
1. Run: 60m (seconds) or	12.0	-	12.8	-
Fast walk: 200m (minutes, seconds)	-	-	-	1:20
400m (minutes, seconds)	-	2:50	-	-
2. Cross-country: 300m (minutes, seconds)	-	-	1:25	-
800m (minutes, seconds) or	3:15	-	-	-
Jogging (minutes)	20	15	10	8
3. Standing long jump: cm	190	170	150	130
4. Grenade throw: 500g (m)	-	-	18	-
700g (m) or	32	-	-	-
Shot-put: 4kg (m,cm)	-	-	5.56	-
7.257kg (m,cm) or	6.20	-	-	-
Stuffed-ball putt: 2kg (m)	-	8	-	6
5. Skiing: 2km (minutes)	-	-	18	time not calculated
5km (minutes)	35	time not calculated	-	-
In snowless regions:				
Jog walk: 3km (minutes)	-	-	25	time not calculated
5km (minutes) or	40	time not calculated	-	-
Cycling: 5km (minutes)	-	-	20	-
10km (minutes)	40	-	-	-
6. Swimming: m (time not taken)	100	50	100	50
7. Push-ups on gym bench from resting position (times)	10	8	6	4
8. Pistol shooting: 25m (hits)	34	-	-	-
9. Hiking: km	20	10	20	10

CHAPTER SIX

The Ice-Hockey Phenomenon

The Russian ice-hockey explosion began in 1950 with Anatoly Tarasov. He is personally responsible for the Soviets' spectacular success in international competition: he originated their training program, which combines Canadian techniques with innovative tactics that are purely Russian. Recognizing that hockey is a team game that requires a high degree of skill, physical conditioning, and desire, the Soviet master coach's program is superior to its North American counterparts in the latter two respects and at least equal to them in the first. The main weapon of Soviet hockey is passing. Passing requires teamwork, which is what Russian hockey is all about. It starts with very definite aims: to involve as many players as possible and to develop an athletic elite.

The methods of achieving these aims are different than those in North America. The Golden Puck concept involves 2½ million boys in two age divisions, 10 to 13 and 14 to 15, and the boys actually start receiving instruction at about age 7.

The Golden Puck competitions are held from September through March, starting at the street level and progressing up to the national championship. There are 16 national titles for 12-year-old teams up to the masters level (over 17) as well as separate competitions for roller-skate hockey. Different teams represent each region every year, and the coaches are all volunteers. Gifted players who attend specialized sports schools cannot play in the Golden Puck. Most are spotted early, before they reach 10 years of age, and are enrolled in specialized sports schools. They play in their own competitions and supply the Olympic and world-caliber teams.

The Central Red Army is a specialized sports school, long famous for its coach Tarasov. A number of coaches at the school have earned the coveted Merited Master of Sport title, which is awarded only to coaches who train Olympic-caliber athletes. The school recruits twice a year, sometimes tapping boys as young as six years of age. There is usually a waiting list of 50 to 60 players—when an opening becomes available, players are given a two-month tryout. The training program begins with a preparatory stage of development for boys from 7 to 11 years of age.

The boys train on the ice three times a week for two hours; the rest of the time they participate in soccer, gymnastics, and other sports in order to develop flexibility and agility.

Only 8 hockey games are played in a year, culminating in the Tarasov Cup. If the 7-year-olds are playing against the 11-year-olds, no body checking is allowed and a goal handicap is given to compensate for the age difference. Boys in this age group train between September and April, attend Pioneer Camps in June and July, and spend August with their parents. Boys 12 to 15 years old are considered to be in the explosive period of development. Their training emphasizes speed and strength, and they work on transfer skills, such as stickhandling and forehand-to-backhand. These boys play 20 games per year, 10 exhibition and 10 league. The 16- to 18-year-olds play 80 games a year and compete for the city, regional, and national titles. In this postadolescent stage of development the boys undergo strenuous physiological and psychological training. They have on-ice practices three to six times a week during the winter and also engage in weight training for half an hour beforehand. Summer training camp runs from June 15 to July 15. The 18- to 19-year-olds play about 100 games per year, ending with final playoffs. The better players try out for the National Team and their sports-school team. Coaches are awarded Certificates of Distinction for preparing athletes capable of playing at the national level. There are ten master's teams in the first division, 14 teams in the second, and 26 in the third.

In the Russian system athletes and coaches ideally work at their sport daily. They are also expected to study subjects that will ensure their future after their playing and/or coaching days are over, a work-study concept that is also familiar in North America.

There are two major differences between the North American just-let-them scrimmage approach and the Russian approach of scientific analysis. The Russians stress passing, teamwork, and puck-control skills—in effect, they play soccer on skates, with attack and counterattack. North Americans place too much stress on shooting, especially the wildly chaotic slap shot. Both believe the center to be the key to any hockey team.

One of the biggest differences in the Soviet approach is the dry-land off-ice conditioning and training program. Skating oneself into shape isn't the Russian way. Conditioning is a prerequisite for later performance. Russian programs are designed to develop all-around body strength and harmony of action.

Cardiorespiratory capacity is the ability to persist in very strenuous tasks. The cardiovascular and respiratory systems have to be built up to keep supplying the working muscles with oxygen. The heart is the key to reducing fatigue. Flexibility is the normal capacity of the joints to move through whatever range of motion is required. Endurance is the ability to persist in localized muscular efforts. Muscular strength is the maximum amount of force that a muscle or muscle group can exert in a single effort.

The Central Red Army trains eleven months of the year to maintain efficiency. Preparation is from July through mid-September. If a given season includes competitions such as the World Cup contests in September 1976 between Finland, Sweden, Canada, Russia, Czechoslovakia, and the United States, training starts in June. Teams play a 44-game league schedule plus Europe Cup, World Competitions, and other tournaments. Some players make the National Team, which competes in Olympic, World Championship, and Canada Cup play. The Soviet schedule normally includes about 80 games, and the players are given a 30- to 40-day mid-season break at a Black Sea resort.

Training usually begins during the first week of July with about 19 hours of off-ice exercises to strengthen individual capacities and abilities. The second week involves 22 hours, the third 19, the fourth 19, and the fifth 19, but the latter three weeks are subject to hourly increases as dictated. The National Hockey League has a 21-day training period, much of which centers around preseason exhibitions among out-of-shape players. Even Team USA started its training for the Canada Cup in August: the first game is held at the beginning of September.

The Russian training session includes a warmup period, agility drills, and circuit training with and without weights. The warmups include such tried-and-true items as jogging, hopping on each foot alternately, running with knees raised as high as possible, running backwards in 360-degree turns with the heels raised, and alternate running and squatting with the arms swinging in a circle. Additional exercises with partners include joining hands and alternately pushing against each other in a seesaw motion, placing hands on shoulders and bending at the waist as far as possible, placing hands on shoulders and kicking the legs as high as possible, facing back-to-back with elbows clasped and alternately bending forward and lifting the partner on the back, and squatting. Sprinting, sideways sprinting, and wind sprints are other variations.

The agility drills comprise jogging with and without obstacles, jumping up while raising the knees up as high as possible, squat jumps with a circular motion, and various types of pushups with partners, such as a wheelbarrow-hookup situation with the man on the bottom doing the pushups, either moving or stationary; in a wheel-barrowhookup position with the bottom man doing hand-clapping-type pushups; or in a fireman's carry with the top man moving in and around the waist of the carrier until he is back in the starting position.

Circuit training without weights includes about ten exercises, such as situps over a bench, with weights or bars holding the feet; squats with one leg extended; situps, lifting both arms and legs to meet above the waist; pushups with a bench at the feet; stepping down from and up to a high bench; with the stomach over a bench or horse and feet held, lifting the head as high as possible and arching the back with the hands in back of the head throughout the exercise; backwards and forwards sprints; sideways obstacle course jumping jacks; and forward-roll series. The exercises with weights include jumping up and down with 100-pound weights on the back; situps over a bend or horse with weights, with the legs held; squats with weights; holding a heavy pipe with a weight like a hockey stick and moving it back and forth as in stickhandling; curls done standing on a bench, with weights picked up from the floor; hopping on both and on each leg with weights held on the shoulders; and a rowing motion with weights. Players are expected to go through both parts of the program about three times with a five-minute rest that includes jogging. The goal is as high as ten to twelve repetitions. After he has finished, the player's pulse is checked for medical analysis.

Vital to the dry-land training program are games other than hockey, such as soccer and basketball (including one-on-one shoulder carries) and strengthening exericses. These exercises have four major objectives: to develop strength with repeated use of heavy weights over a short period of time; to develop movement strength with weighted pucks; to develop con-

Russia has made a habit of winning the Hockey Gold Medal since 1952, with only the United States' surprise win in 1960 preventing a succession of Soviet triumphs.

trolled, directed strength with elastic wrist drills; and to develop endurance with weights carried on the body during practice sessions.

On-ice conditioning and training during the preparation period lasts about two hours with 30 players taking part, usually including about 5 younger players (16-18 years old). These sessions prepare each player for the competitive period. Stress is placed upon developing power and mobility on the ice. Exercises include skating with weights on the body, skating against the pull of a rubber cable, and shooting or passing while the arms or body or both is restrained by an elastic device. Fundamentals are mastered long before exercises are attempted.

Russian skating techniques are more ankle- than hip-oriented. Tarasov feels that Canadian professionals sometimes take off improperly, lift the foot too high after takeoff, return the blade to the ice too abruptly, use too much hip movement, and have generally weak muscles. Soviet players do not lace their skates to the top in order to permit freer ankle movements. They don't have weak ankles after their training program. Soviet techniques also include gliding rather than pushing the blade to the ice and a more angular style of backward skating than forward skating.

Drills include keeping blades on the ice; jumping over obstacles with alternate legs, and skating around the rink along the boards, taking a forward roll, and returning quickly to a skating position. Stickhandling drills are used frequently, such as the time-honored forwards-versus-the-defense, with the defense playing without sticks and trying to take the puck away with their skates. Receiving the puck is taught by having pairs of players constantly pass to each other while cushioning the puck and by having players receive a pass from the corner of the rink in full stride and shoot at the goal. The development of shooting skills centers around aiming weighted pucks at moving and stationary targets. The Russians do not believe in the slap shot because it is less accurate and tips off the goalie. In a wrist shot the player can look at the target peripherally; in a slap shot he must look down at the puck.

The Russians use dry-land field-hockey sticks and balls to vary their training.

The Soviets have a special off-ice conditioning program for the goaltender. Efficient lateral movements are a must, along with great concentration. Tarasov and most Russian coaches still feel that Russian goaltending is far behind North American standards. Vladislav Tretiak was the exception who enabled the Soviets to tie Team Canada NHL and beat Team Canada WHA, but he really is the exception! Many say that Czechoslovakia's Jiri

Holocek is the best goalie in the world—better than Bernie Parent, Ken Dryden, or Tony Esposito.

Russian coaches feel that the goalie needs special attention and realize that he is the most important man on the team. They have initiated off-ice programs that are performed in standard gym suits with catching and blocker gloves and standard goal stick. Tennis balls, racquets, weights, medicine balls, volleyballs, and basketballs are used in the exercises, which include basic conditioning, gymnastics, general conditioning, weight training, recreation, and screening drills.

In a program designed for one instructor and two goalies the basic conditioning exercises are: running laps around the gym while bouncing a tennis ball for five minutes; running while bouncing two tennis balls; bouncing on one leg in a squat position while throwing the other leg in a butterfly motion; and alternating legs while bouncing a tennis ball. Another exercise is for one goalie to carry another on his back while skating around the gym. Broad jumping from a squat position develops explosive power in the upper leg area, as does jumping to a standing position from a squat position.

Gymnastics include front rolls on a standard mat while a tennis ball is hit toward the player from about fifteen feet; leaping front rolls in which the goalie must catch the ball and go into another roll; regular front and back rolls in which the goalie must jump up with legs spread and knees bent before going into another roll; diving over a chair, onto a mat, and into a front roll while catching a ball hit with a tennis racquet; the same exercise but catching the ball while diving over the chair. This part of the program ends with two-man-chain front rolls in which the ankles of each goalie are grasped by his partner.

In the general and specific conditioning programs goalies stand about five feet from a wall with a tennis ball in each hand and throw them at the wall and catch them on the rebound. Goalies throw a medicine ball and a volleyball back and forth to each other in a squatting position and play soccer with the medicine ball, one attacking and one defending. They also play soccer with a tennis ball, which is much smaller and harder to control and build up reflexes. In another exercise a goalie with a stick and gloves stands in front of a wood netlike area and defends against tennis balls hit at him from about 15 feet. They are aimed at low stick side, low glove side, high glove side, high stick side, and mixed. The idea is for the goalie to prevent rebounds by either clearing or catching the tennis balls. This exercise is also done from long-range distances of about 30 to 35 feet.

In a purely Soviet drill the instructor stands between two goalies and swings his racquet high and low. The goalies are required to jump over low swings and duck under high swings. Two goalies also face each other at arms' length in the butterfly position and throw tennis balls back and forth. Using both forehand and backhand, both goalies pass a medicine ball back and forth to each other. They also kick a tennis ball back and forth from a distance of about ten to twelve feet. With both goalies in a butterfly position and an arm's length apart, the instructor drops a tennis ball between them and the goalies attempt to capture it.

This phase is followed by a five-minute rest period, after which weight training is performed. Ten pounds on the back end of the bar is the usual requirement. With a barbell resting across his back the goalie must jump up and down into deep knee bends. This is repeated while moving forward. Two goalies throw the barbell back and forth underhand and overhand. A weight is placed in the goalie's stick hand and he simulates blocking a high shot while bouncing a tennis ball with his glove hand and vice versa.

The Soviets have recreational drills with tennis balls, including goalie-screening drills, which North American professionals scarcely ever practice. The goalie practices with two other men, a stationary screening player and an instructor who hits a tennis ball past the screening player. The screening player can vary his distance from the goalie and even try to block or deflect the shot—shades of Gary Dornhoefer, Camille Henry, or Tony Leswick. The shooter also varies his distance, and the goalie must get used to the sudden changes in direction. Russian goalies start this curriculum at the age of ten: most Canadians and Americans don't even know what position they will play. The squatting gymnastic approach differs from the NHL and WHA theory that a stand-up position blocking the angles is the best for the goalie. Going down puts a goalie at the mercy of the shooter according to accepted NHL theory; the Russians don't disagree completely but still believe in the squat position and a gymnast in the nets.

Soviet on-the-ice training isn't that **different from North American practice. A teacher or trainer verbally explains a skill and demonstrates it in toto and step-by-step. The player then tries to execute the whole movement, and** the teacher analyzes the step-by-step action. Correction and adjustment are made by both. The Russians make extensive use of videotape even at low age levels and encourage the students to analyze their own work. Ages 7 to 11 are in the preparatory stage; 12 to 14, growth and acceleration of skills; 15 and up critical analysis and physical training.

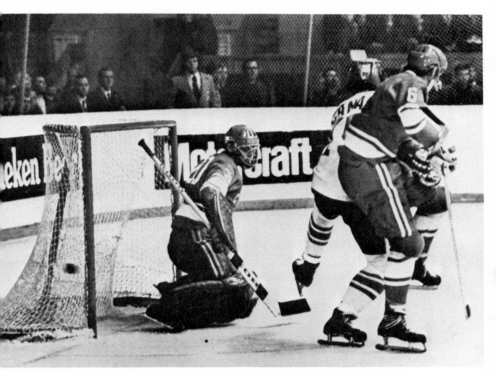

Goalie Vladislav Tretiah is the most famous Russian hockey player.

All coaches, Russian and North American, agree that skating is the name of the game, and it is the basis upon which the Central Red Army and National teams play hockey. The main starting position involves tucking the stomach under to ease the operation of the heart and lungs. The head is up, and the knees are slightly bent. The player can choose either a high, level, or low stance, which is usually dictated by the length of the stick. The pushing leg extends out at a 45- to 60-degree angle. At the start of the stride the ankle is at a 65- to 75-degree angle and opens up as much as 120 degrees at the final push. Soviet players use their hips more than Canadians, who skate far more upright. The Russians, Finns, Czechs, and Swedes skate with their heads further forward than do the North Americans. Because of the Soviets' low, crouching position the upper body can be held higher, giving them a better overall view of the rink and helping their famed passing game. The Soviets make more long passes up the middle from defensemen to teammates in the neutral zone than do any of their opponents.

Canadian players skate with their legs wide apart, ready for instant body contact. This makes for shorter strides and slower getaway. Europeans skate with more jumps and longer gliding strokes. The Canadians can manage sharp turns at full speed better because of their spread-leg style. For sheer speed, as opposed to starts and stops, the Soviet player can catch up to or skate away from an opponent better with his style of skating. The starting point of the thrust is not as far away from his foot as it is with the average North American. Russians lean into turns, whereas the North Americans counterbalance by leaning the other way. The Russian analysis of backward skating for the beginner revolves around the center of gravity. Most players don't crouch correctly and are simply thrown backwards. It is vital that the support leg doesn't go past the center of gravity. The pushing foot must be even with the center of gravity, or the player falls. Again, the angle of the body depends upon the stick that the player uses.

Tarasov considers starting as the main weapon in skating because of the time gained by a quick start. At the beginning of the takeoff the strides, especially the first two, must be short and sharp. The next step is to increase speed quickly, especially when guarded unexpectedly, as do Gordie Howe, Robby Orr or the Soviet's Valery Kharlamòv. There are about 150 to 200 stops during a game, so practice must be harder—about 250 stops.

In practice the Russians vary their skating, the forwards becoming defensemen in one-on-one situations. How many times in an NHL game does a forward, usually the point on the power play, surrender a goal because he can't handle just such a skating situation?

The Soviets also do a number of gymnastic skating exercises, in which jumping, roll-over and fall-down drills are the mode. The Russians' famous rubber-cable device is also attached to the dashers. The player skates away from the boards, meeting more and more resistance as he skates. At any point, both expected and unexpected, the coach can pull the cable, which results in a shock and jerk not unlike an unexpected body check.

Skating without stickhandling would accomplish very little. NHL history is replete with classic skaters who failed because they didn't master the other techniques of the game. The stick can be held two ways (left-handed or right-handed), and the Russians teach players to stickhandle in front, at the side, and in a diagonal position. Most players hold their sticks in the left hand: using a right-handed player on the right wing can help ward off the opposition when he cuts in on the goal. His free left hand can hold off the defenseman.

In teaching the dribble the Russians keep the blade perpendicular to the surface, with a short side-to-side dribble. As a player gets older and presumably more experienced and better, the length of the dribble can be longer. At all times the player watches the ice ahead of him and controls the puck with feel or peripheral vision. The Russians use the wide dribble, which is borrowed from their game of bandy, when they need speed or are in a wide-open situation. Many Soviet drills involve stickhandling through cones placed at alternate distances on the ice. The Soviets realize the importance of simultaneous movement of hands and feet and train with situps while stickhandling, first with the puck to the side and then with the puck between the legs.

The Russians have analyzed the most effective passes in the various ice zones and practice them ad infinitum. They believe in three basic passes: longitudinal, diagonal, and across. Tarasov believes that there are seven main ingredients in passing: (1) pass smoothly and quickly, camouflaging if possible; (2) make the puck spin; (3) follow the puck as you receive it and always try to increase speed the moment you take it in; (4) as puck carrier put yourself in a position so that you can see as many of your fellow players as possible; (5) always pass to those who are in a better position and who are moving faster than you are; (6) never pass sideways unnecessarily, especially in the offensive zone—instead use the backwards drop pass; (7) make your passes as convenient as possible for the recipient. In the NHL only the Montreal Canadiens, with their fire-wagon approach and technique of headmanning the puck to the player nearest the opposition's goal, come close to the Soviet pass strategy. In the 1972 Team Canada-Russia series the Soviets attempted almost twice as many passes as the Canadians. The Russians use an assembly-line technique in passing drills, with players lined up at short and long distances apart. The motions of the arms and legs as well as the cushioning of the puck during reception are emphasized. As players get better, the speed and tempo are increased.

In shooting the Russians place great value on speed, accuracy, and quickness of release. The positioning of the lower hand in the wrist shot depends on the strength of the shooter: the thumb hand is usually about one-third down the shaft. The Russians believe that the best stick have most of their weight in the handle, with flexible, thin blades with a curvature of about ½ to 1 cm. The curved blade used now in the WHA and formerly used in the NHL prohibits puck control, although it creates dipping and curving shots.

The hardest shot is made when the puck is positioned in the center of the blade. Many Soviet players cut an inch off the end of the blade, which forces them to use the center. The toe is the best for a quick snap shot, but the middle is the only spot for slapping the puck or blasting a slap shot. The power of a slap shot is determined by the relation of the puck to the support leg at the point of impact. The puck must be at the inside heel of the support leg and as close to the body as possible.

Soviet methods stress locking the blade when shooting, which means using the thumb of the upper hand and the strength of the lower. The Russians develop release speed by using lighter pucks, which enables players to work on quickness. To develop power, they use weighted pucks. For accuracy both moving and stationary targets are employed. Moving targets force the shooter to look at the target and control the puck with peripheral vision.

Soviet methods involve sweep shot, wrist shot, and slap shot, with the latter used only from a distance and when the goalie is partially screened. The sweep shot begins, if the player is left-handed, when the stick begins to move forward. The wrists are tightened, and the body weight is moved to the lead foot—the right foot in a left-handed player. The puck should be in the middle of the blade, with the hands gripping the stick tightly but not too far apart. The wrist shot calls for strength in the wrist and lower arms. The

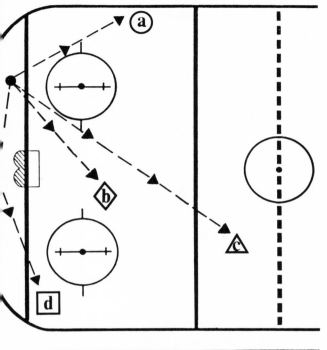

Defensive zone break out passes:

A - Pass to winger on boards.

B - Pass to center for basketball give and go.

C - Breakaway pass.

D - Behind the net pass.

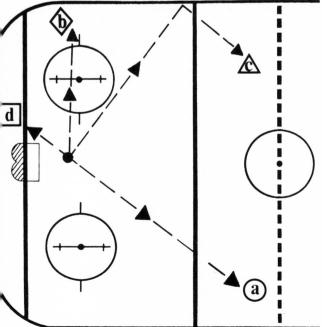

When clearing from slot area:

A - Between defense to opposite side wing.

B - Clearance to boards

C - Off the boards to winger

D - Behind net to ease heavy pressure

player uses this shot if he is close. He must make the backward-forward movement of the blade as fast as possible; his upper body, arms, and wrist must be relaxed until the exact moment when the stick makes contact with the puck; and he must follow through with the puck on the blade as far as possible. Most Soviet players use a combined sweep-wrist shot, with the wrist shot being favored in close. In the wrist shot the blade gives strength. Rocket Rchard used it, as did Jean Beliveau, both of whom never used the slap shot. Anatoly Firsov, the Soviet Grand Master, used the wrist shot. In modern play Aleksandr Yakushev, Boris Mikhailov, Aleksandr Maltsev, and Valeri Kharlamov all use the wrist and sweep shots, with only a rare slap shot. Phil Esposito believes in getting his wrist shot off as quickly as possible. The 210-pound Espo stands in the slot, the area directly in front of the net, and simply shoots immediately upon receipt of the puck. From the point Bobby Orr believes in a modified slap-wrist shot in which he doesn't raise the stick very far back and follows through with the blade. Bobby Hull and Stan Mikita introduced the slap shot in the NHL, and through international play it influenced the European concept. Hull's 120 mph canonball was simply a perfection of the Boom Boom Geoffrion slapper of the early 1950s. John Mayasich, who remained an amateur when the NHL had only six teams but would easily command a six-figure salary today, believed that the slap shot was a great attack weapon. The slap shot is taken by raising the stick as far behind as possible and golfing it at the net. The stick should strike the ice behind the puck. This bends the stick like a crossbow and puts more force into the shot. Anatoly Firsov developed his slap shot with a shorter stick than Hull uses. Most NHL players can fire the slap shot on the move better than the Soviets, but this is slowly changing. The backhand shot is rarely seen in this NHL era of fire-wagon power hockey, but in the scientific Russian approach it is still the same key weapon that it was when Beliveau was using it to great effect. Gordie Howe, who is ambidextrous, used backhanders frequently and still surprises today with an occasional backhand-flip shot.

In North America the sweep pass is the most frequently taught. In the Soviet Union the emphasis is on the snap pass or wrist pass, which can be made while stickhandling. The Soviets use the time-honored technique of boarding up a net and marking off six basic areas in the corners to shoot at, with the greatest emphasis on the two lower corners.

Despite North American opinion, the Soviets body-check quite well, but they do lag behind the NHL in this respect, because many of the offensive and defensive tactics of their hockey are borrowed from soccer and bandy,

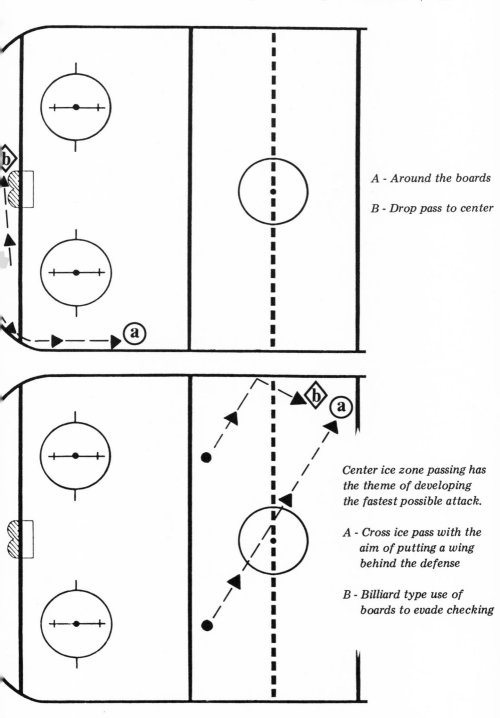

A - Around the boards

B - Drop pass to center

Center ice zone passing has the theme of developing the fastest possible attack.

A - Cross ice pass with the aim of putting a wing behind the defense

B - Billiard type use of boards to evade checking

which is a game played on a frozen field with skates, sticks, and a ball. The Russians are physically strong, but they lack the techniques to deliver body checks. They have attempted to improve by taping the various Team Canada-Russia series and analyzing the action. There are four aspects of body checking: the moment of impact, center of gravity, position of supporting leg, and choice of position. The best time to make contact is when the opponent's attention is directed elsewhere. The center of gravity should be lower than the opponent's, which requires the checker to crouch slightly, and he must straddle or spread his legs so that his support is greater. The Russians work at one-on-one situations—and practice having the defenseman ride or hip-check the attacker wide or into the boards. This is the same as the Canadian system. Although the Russians prescribe checking in the slot area in front of the net, not much is realy done there in comparison to the guerrilla warfare that takes place in front of an NHL net. If Esposito were left unguarded in the slot, as players are in European hockey, he might have made a record 100 goals instead of his record 76. The Soviets still haven't resolved the problem of whether to relax or roll with a check when hit or to tense up and fight the check.

Russian team tactics work on the theory of five-man units, with the same sets of defensemen always working with the same forward line. The Russians basically guard one-on-one in the defensive end, with the slot more open than in the NHL. If a player is beaten and an opponent skates into the slot, it can allow a dangerous shot on goal. The Soviets also employ a five-man-zone defense in the defensive end, in which one man never moves from the slot area. The other four players cover interacting zones. When tow offensive players are in the corner with the puck, the Soviet system calls for one defenseman to chase with the help of the center. The center must be mobile enough to skate from one side of the rink to the other to keep up with the puck. Sometimes both defensemen go in the corner, and the center picks up the slot. This is a no-no in the NHL. In the five-man system the five men become almost interchangeable, something that doesn't happen with the two sets of defensemen and three forward lines normally used in North American hockey. On attack the Russians hope for two-on-one, three-on-one, and go in very deep, but they are picked up by the wingers far more than in the NHL.

In penalty killing the Russians use the standard folding box in the defensive zone when they are short a man. One defenseman handles the corner,

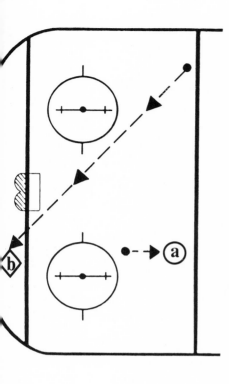

(Top) Offensive zone passing shows the Soviet at their best.

A - The simple drop pass to a skater follow- ing the puck carrier. The first skater leaves the puck behind and runs interference by skating into the defender.

B - Cross ice pass designed to hit winger on the fly in goal mouth area.

(Bottom left) Offensive zone point passing by defense.

A - To the corner

B - To the slot

C - To the opposite side wing

D - Cross ice to the other point

(Below) Offensive zone give and go in which the defenseman at the point passes to the corner and then breaks to the slot for return pass.

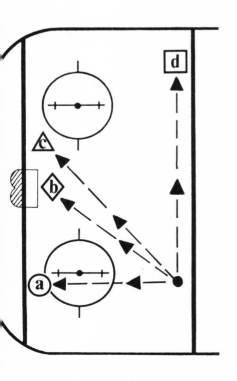

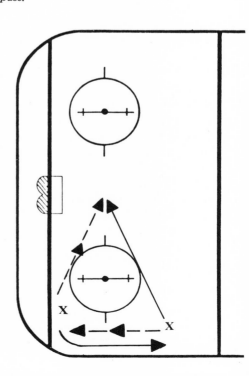

the other the slot, and the two forwards rotate from the slot to the points. If they are two men short, the Russians use the North American triangle, but it is very disciplined. The three defenders don't move too far from the goal. Two men try to pack the puck no matter where it is, and the third is away from the puck. The NHL tries to pick off the man at the top of the triangle. The Russians' discipline sometimes shortcircuits this. Sometimes the Russians use three defensemen in the triangle.

On a power play it is important to remember that the right wingers almost always make off-shots—lefthand shots a la Richard. The winger must be good at handling the puck on his backhand, something the Reds practice constantly. The Reds like to place two men in the same corner in a power-play situation. This puts pressure on the defense and helps to gain possession. They try to expand this two-on-one corner situation to a two-on-one slot situation and a resultant shot on goal. The idea is to reduce the five-on-four to two-on-one with the option of passing to the point. The Russians use the five-man diamond attack on a power play in which the point man heads straight for the net hoping for a pass from the corners. The two wingers line up near the sides of the goal and scramble for a rebound. The options are numerous. With two men in front the point man could either shoot or pass. Since the defending team has at most only one man in the slot, the diamond would have cracked the box. With a two-man advantage the Rusians try to send in two big wingmen to tie up the defense and enable the point or center to shoot from the slot.

The Russians have various drills to implement their training and tactical programs. One is jumping over obstacles, sometimes sticks laid at a point on the ice. The players jump over them, landing on either one or two knees, and then jump up, sometimes with a quick pivot before jumping. The Russians place cones at the blue and red lines and skate through them to develop their skating agility. They sometimes place cones very deep in the corners, which forces their wingers to get used to them. The players skate around a face-off circle, with one leg always gliding on the ice and the other leg pushing off. They also use a variety of relay races.

Although their background in soccer obviously helps, the Russians use their feet better than do most NHL players. In one drill two players without sticks start at the boards equidistant from a puck in mid-ice. Whichever players gets to it first must foot-handle the puck and work his way back to his boards. Sometimes the Reds will play a game without sticks and without goalies. At other times they vary this with three men against three. They also go three-on-three with only the offensive players having sticks or five-on-three drills with only the defensive group having sticks.

In passing drills the Russians sometimes run three-on-none drills with as many as three pucks, trying to maintain constant skating speed and throwing the pucks back and forth. They vary this with two-on-nones in and out of cones placed in strategic spots. The Russians try long, longitudinal passes in their breakout patterns from their own end. They station wingers along the boards and two defensemen behind the net. The defensemen pass the puck back and forth, and when the winger breaks, the defenseman hits him with a pass at about the red line. By adding a defenseman at the blue line the pass must be accurate, and the winger must elude the defender. The Russians work on their passing and shooting with multiple pucks. Players skate into the slot and receive passes from either corner. They must receive the puck and shoot in one motion. The Russians work two-man teams in rebound drills, in which the original shooter goes into the corner. This drill is interesting and also helps conditioning. The Soviets have also sorts of variations on these drills, with special emphasis on the drop pass.

They practice skating, stickhandling, and shooting at the same time with six cones on the ice. The player must circle the cones in full stride and finish off by shooting the puck at the net. Sometimes a defenseman just past the last cone tries to check each attacker. The usual Canadian stops and starts are also employed. Stickhandling drills, mostly using one-on-one situations with a variety of checking techniques, are prevalent.

Sometimes six defensemen are set up inside the blue line. The single attack player carries the puck over the line, and each defenseman takes a shot at him. They can do anything legal to stop him. When the attacking player is stopped, he must go back and start over. He must beat at least two men: he is never allowed to throw the puck in and forget it, as the NHL players often do. Using a face-off circle, the Russians place five men on the perimeter and one in the middle at the face-off spot. The outside five pass constantly to each other, while the inside man attempts to intercept the passes. When he succeeds, the player he beat has to step into the middle of the circle.

CHAPTER SEVEN

Why the Soviet Way Works

It is a simple fact that must be accepted: the U.S.S.R. is the most physically fit nation in the world. In the last quarter-century, the Soviet Union has established physical education, culture, and health programs that are unmatched in any other country. It took a lot of money, time, and effort, but no one in the Soviet sports system can or would have any reason to doubt the results.

The Russian sports organization is unsurpassed. Although it has some drawbacks, especially in its programs for less talented youngsters, the sports schools and institutes offer a remarkable testimony to the importance of physical education in a country's overall health and status.

Methods for developing coaches in the Soviet Union are excellent: people who train athletes in Russia are true experts in their fields. If there is a way to extract maximum effort from an athlete—and maximum results—the Soviet coach will find it.

The dedication to the development of new training techniques and a physically fit populace is unwavering. The establishment of the G.T.O. and the P.W.D., centralized programs for athletic achievement in everyday life, is exemplary, as is the relationship between work and athletics. Factory sponsorship of physical-education programs is a significant factor in the athletic superiority of the Russians.

Borrowing aspects of foreign sports systems and refining them to fit the Soviet mold is a contributing factor to their overall supremacy on the athletic fields. The Soviets understand that the rest of the world can contribute to their own development as a sporting nation, and they readily accept expertise. Where would Russian hockey be without Canadian help, or Russian basketball without American help—even if that help is inadvertent. Most important, perhaps, is the realization on the part of the Russians that science can be applied to sports. The Soviets readily accepted this fact, established programs in which the sciences regulated athletic progress, and have been rewarded by their faith.

Machines such as a muscle stimulator to enhance muscle production during play are an important part of the Soviet sports system. Their advanced data-gathering programs are enviable. It seems that the Soviet Union has a scientific or medical explanation for every facet of sports and a way to cope with the athlete's problems, both physical and psychological.

Not all is perfection in the Soviet sports community. At the international level, the inability of the participant to enjoy himself should be criticized. More than anything sports should be fun, and in the U.S.S.R., which encourages passionless performance, it is not fun. It is mostly work, hard work. The Russian athlete has little outlet for his emotions. He must learn to subjugate them—not necessarily the key to athletic success. Despite what the Soviet sports hierarchy may think, emotions cannot always be replaced with skill.

Russian supremacy as a sports power is predicated on teaching the young people and strictly regimenting the potential stars in the Communist way. Should politics play such an important part in world sports competition? Probably not, but the Russians get favorable results, so why change?

On the home front the Soviet people are well conditioned physically, with little politics involved. This is important. The Soviet Union likes to brag about its accomplishments in international competition, but it is at home, among the masses, that the sports programs are most enviable. The percentage of outstanding athletes that a nation develops is small. The general health of the populace should take preference.

Dr. Henry Morton, in his book *Soviet Sports*, made the following assessment of the Russian program:

The Soviet advance has, of course, been no historical accident; it could not be in a state where the ruling elite believes in history for a purpose. By operating a comprehensive, centrally controlled, heavily subsidized sport program; by coaching selected athletes in the latest methods gathered from domestic and foreign experiences in special sport schools and at climactically favorable training sites for long periods; and by offering them material rewards, prestige, opportunities beyond their sport prime (on a parallel with other privileged groups in Soviet society), they have achieved a glowing Olympic and international sport record.

1112-5-SB
5-17